LEADING WITH EASE

Creating a Solid Foundation for Your Leadership Role

Lisa Wilson

D1728226

Published by
Hybrid Global Publishing
333 E 14th Street
#3C
New York, NY 10003

Manufactured in the United States of America, or in the United Kingdom when distributed elsewhere.

Wilson, Lisa.
Leading With Ease
    ISBN: 9781957013541
    eBook: 9781957013558
    LCCN: 2022917560

Cover design by: Natasha Clawson
Copyediting by: Barbra Conway
Interior design by: Suba Murugan
Author photo by: Aurele Monfils

https://lmwcoaching.ca
https://leadingwithease.ca

Contents

Putting It All Together   99

Foreword

Leadership is EVERYTHING.

Well, maybe not everything.

But good leaders help the home to run a lot more smoothly. Good leaders allow the office to run more smoothly as well.

Good leaders help the team accomplish more, and feel better doing it.

Good leaders typically have followers who are more excited to follow them down basically any path or maybe even any alley.

Good leaders often have good followers.

I recall one time hearing a wise leadership expert say, "If you're a leader [say, in the office] with no followers, you're really just taking a walk [around the office, or on the streets]."

The challenge is it's not easy to be a good leader. It's even harder than it was before.

When I was growing up, people either thought someone was a good manager, or they weren't. We didn't even really use the word *leader*. Everything was encompassed in the word *manager*.

Today, though, we realize managers and leaders are different things—and both do exist.

A good manager doesn't necessarily make a good leader.

Although, ironically, a good leader often makes a good manager.

Paradigm?

Either way, the traits of a manager and leader, in my opinion, are vastly different, and it is that difference that makes it so rare to find a good leader.

Now, I'm not going to spend pages telling you all of the traits, in my opinion, of a good leader because Lisa Wilson has done a marvelous job exploring leadership in such a great way in this very book.

I will say, though, that I think good leaders are good communicators, good at sharing their vision, and good at bringing everyone together within that vision. They also believe in the importance of the team and work to make their team stronger, they aim to create a culture where everyone wins together, and they often won't assign work they would never be willing to do themselves.

Oh, and they never let the team fail alone.

I have had to learn many of these skills the hard way. I wish I had a book like *Leading with Ease* when I was just starting out. Imagine how much time I could have saved and how much further along I might be. What I love about this book is it gives you the foundation of solid leadership, and far too many people build things on weak foundations.

The good news is that now that you have access to this book, your leadership skillsand approach will be built on a solid foundation.

What I also love about this book is how it focuses on the person, you, first. Just like building on a weak foundation, I feel that if you don't work on you first, and many don't, none of the rest matters.

I used to deliver sales training weekly. So many of the salespeople who took the training wanted to jump ahead to the secrets, the strategies, and the sales techniques.They would complain that I began by talking about them, the person, and teaching soft personal skills, and having them take a personal inventory of where they were at currently, and that I spoke of personal development, and so on.

I would have to slow them down and make them realize that if they aren't the right person yet, or they aren't ready yet, none of the sales techniques and skills would matter.

I applaud this book for doing the same—versus the more popular approach of jumping right into techniques and leadership strategies.

On that note, I'm known for not writing many forewords, and I say no regularly when asked.

Watching Lisa as a client, seeing her speak on our bLU Talks stage, and knowing her work as a fellow community member, I know firsthand her ability to help people improve their leadership foundation, and as a result, when she humbled me by asking if I would write this foreword, I knew fairly quickly I would be writing it.

If you plan to become a successful modern leader, *Leading with Ease* might just be the most important book you read this year.

For some, it may be the most important leadership book you'll ever read.

For that reason, read it. Study it. Share it. I think you'll be thankful you did.

Until then, here's to your Greater Success,
Corey Poirier
Founder, bLU Talks

Introduction

It was one of those moments—you know the ones, they seem like a regular moment, but they are ingrained in your head. I remember it vividly, sitting next to my friend who I used to meet for coffee before our class and introducing myself, being the odd one out in the room again. What the group leader said seemed like a simple sentence, but it would turn out to change the course of my career.

I went to university for psychology; it became clear after my first year that wasn't where I wanted to be. The careers I could have with a psychology degree all required that I spend more time in school, and I was eager to get my life started. School wasn't a long-term goal of mine. Most of the people I met in first year were in business and their courses sounded interesting and with a business degree I felt my options were better. Even though business was never something I'd considered when deciding to go to university, I switched majors. I loved psychology, so I kept taking the courses as my electives.

It was always funny when I got into my psychology class seminar, and we started introducing ourselves. Around the room everyone would say their name and their major. The first person would be a psychology major, the second a sociology major, and it would go back and forth like that until it got to me, and I laughed and said, "Business major." On this particular day, I think the group leader felt bad for me and she said, "You will find a way to mix the two." A short sentence that impacted my life in so many ways. I'll never forget that moment. Prior to that it had never occurred to me that I could mix them; psychology and business felt so far apart in the courses that I was taking. What they were teaching me in economics and math had little to do with psychology. Very shortly afterward I took my first human resources course called Organizational Behavior, and it felt like a repeat of my first-year psychology course. *I found how to mix the two!* I then started taking *all* the human resources courses, and I loved them too.

Getting a job in Human Resources (HR) didn't turn out to be as easy as choosing it as a profession. Everyone wanted experience, so I took a job in HR during my last summer of school. It didn't turn out to be an easy job, but I got through it and hoped that would help me get a job when I finished school. *Nope . . .* everyone still wanted more experience. I wasn't accepting that, and my drive had me keep searching for those elusive HR roles, I managed to get four six-month contracts in a row before finally getting my first full-time role. At that point I decided I would be a human resources manager by the time I was thirty.

Through all these roles, I worked with some amazing leaders and some not-so-great ones. Thankfully in my full-time role I had a wonderful manager/role model who taught me a lot. She was such a great person that I even felt safe telling her that I had been offered a human resources manager's role and turned it down because I didn't think I was ready. She wasn't angry with me for having applied elsewhere; instead she understood my drive, and worked with me to make sure I would be ready the next time I got a similar offer. She told me I needed to work on my "business writing" and my public speaking skills. I found a college that had a "business communications" course close by and joined Toastmasters. The course was done in a couple of months, but public speaking skills took a little longer to hone. I managed to complete the first levels of leadership and communications within a year. My public speaking skills had improved immensely.

In the meantime, my awesome leader put me in positions and on projects that allowed me to learn and grow as a leader. She also let people at head office know that I was interested in moving forward and they tried to find me roles within the company to grow. Unfortunately, the timing was bad; they were trying to move me into the United States shortly after 9/11, and it was harder than usual to get people to work across the border at that time. When the job I turned down came back up, I took it. One year later! I was twenty-eight, and I met my goal a year and a half before my self-imposed deadline.

There I had another great leader, who also recognized my drive and started training me to be a general manager. He, too, put me on projects that allowed me to grow as a leader, including a company-wide project put together to change our safety culture. This wasn't going to be a small project, but I was invited in on the ground floor (see chapter 13 for the full story).

While I was blessed with some great managers, I also had some who were not so great. One female manager said to me once, "My concern for you is that you will have babies and ruin your career." What the . . . ? We were working at a company that was incredibly supportive of both mothers and fathers taking leave after having children. I had another manager wait until the third month of my four-month role to tell me that she felt I was frequently late. I was twenty minutes early every morning. The worst was working at a company who told me during the interview that they needed people with new ideas, but when I started to share my ideas, they told me to "assimilate."

The last one really took its toll. I was constantly told I was wrong. My boss argued with me for twenty minutes one time and then said, "Well, I don't know about that, but we always do it this way." Things I had been praised for in my previous roles, at this company got me into trouble. There was an employee that bullied everyone. When I went to discipline him for his behavior, I was told I needed my boss's approval first, something I'd never needed in any previous management positions. Worse, I did not get it. Instead, I was told to "form a relationship." I did not; this person was bullying management and employees, and no one would deal with his behavior. I was not going to put myself in the way of that type of treatment, especially when my rights as a manager had been taken away. I stayed in this role for three years because I'd moved to a smaller community and bought a house. There were not a lot of options for human resources manager roles, and I was single and had to pay the mortgage.

Three years at a company that did not match my values took its toll. I became a person I didn't recognize, making decisions I would never have made previously and will never make again. Getting up in the morning was difficult. I was doing P90X and CrossFit to manage my high levels of stress, and I started a side business doing some coaching just to have something to look forward to. I was having odd illnesses. When I went to get them checked, there was nothing wrong. Finally, my doctor recognized what was happening and told me that I either took a vacation or he would put me off on stress leave. I chose the vacation and went on a five-day yoga retreat. It wasn't enough! Finally, the company did a restructuring and combined my role with another area. Phew! I got to leave! When I left the role, I was burned out had a lump on my thyroid that needed to be removed. The surgery and subsequent exhaustion are a story I share in other books:

- *Her Global Voice, Feminine Leaders Sharing Their Story to Change and Empower Your Heart, Soul and Spirit*
- *Heal, Vol. 2, You Have the Power*
- *Business, Life and the Universe, Vol. 3*

I knew when I left that role that I would move into my coaching business full time and my goal had always been to coach leaders, but I didn't realize how bad I would be affected by working there. After working there for three years and being constantly told I was wrong, I questioned my ability to coach leaders. I still started to coach, but I focused only on Life Coaching. I wanted nothing to do with human resources or leaders for quite some time, even while I had people I'd previously worked with calling me and saying, "Lisa, you are amazing at this; don't leave the field." My confidence had been shaken, and I couldn't bring myself anywhere near leadership in any way.

While coaching for "life" is a part in all coaching, I didn't have a specific niche for life coaching and consequently my marketing was all over the place, and I didn't bring in a lot of business.

A few years later, I had another one of those moments you don't forget. An amazing friend said to me, "Lisa, you light up when you talk about leadership!" I knew then it was time to go back to working with leaders. That's when I created the course that this book is based on and started flirting with the idea of writing a book.

Throughout my career and since, I've watched leaders struggle, either unsure of what to say or do in situations, which often caused them not to act at all. No action is worse than making a mistake. If you make a mistake, you can ask for forgiveness and do better next time, but when you don't act at all, you don't learn, and your team doesn't have the direction they need.

In the fifteen years I worked in human resources, I took so many leadership courses. Some I took twice or more. I even got to be involved in the creation of the course at one of the companies. They wanted to change their culture and brought a group of us together to help create a framework on how that would be done. I have two shelves full of binders left over after I have more than once gone through them all to get rid of the ones that I no longer needed.

I created the "Leading with Ease" course from the four themes that I felt were the most important from all the training I'd taken. Those same themes are what we will review in this book.

While I loved receiving training, there were a couple of things that I took issue with. First, they took me away from work for days at a time. I learned great things but didn't have time to integrate them. As I'm sure you have felt before, the moment I returned to work, I was so busy catching up from what I'd missed on the days I was away that the binder got thrown up on the shelf and forgotten.

The next piece was that each course only discussed one topic in depth. For a new leader, this would take months to get all the information they needed, and in the meantime they were left to flounder.

With the course, and now the book, I want leaders to have all the foundational pieces, or roots, in one place.

- *To know and understand yourself and those around you better.* Understand your strengths and know that they are strengths, even if they haven't always been celebrated as such.

- *To know and appreciate your team for the strengths that they have, even if those strengths make it difficult for you to communicate with them.* Of course, once you are aware of both of those things to use everyone's strengths to the fullest, remembering to celebrate your differences.

- *To be clear on where you are going, how you will get there and what behaviors are off limits in this process.* The clearer you are on these pieces, the easier it is to make decisions when you are faced with a tough situation. It will also help you to communicate your vision and expectations to your team. When they are clear, they spend way less time checking in because they know what decisions to make on their own.

- *To know your role and be confident in it.* Research on new leaders suggests that one of the biggest concerns for a new leader is how they add value to the company. They feel busy all day, running around to this meeting and that one, answering all the questions, but there is nothing tangible at the end of the day that they can say they completed. In their previous role they knew they did a great job because of the number of parts they had completed or the spreadsheet or document they completed, or the quality of their work. For a leader those tangibles aren't there. Your success is measured by the moral of the team, how well it's functioning, and the quality of your team's production. All of these are measured over a longer period of time, and at the end of a hard day, no one is there to remind you that your team worked together amazingly through whatever crisis you dealt with, and that's your "production."

- *Finally, feeling confident in having those difficult conversations in a way that will ensure everyone feels safe sharing their personal experience in every situation, while continuing to hold the values and expected behaviors.* It's never fun to have these conversations, but without them your team won't function as well.

When I created the course, I wanted new leaders to have the foundation they needed all in one place. What I discovered was that leaders who had been in the role for several years were the ones primarily signing up. They had been in their roles for some time, but no one had ever put together a foundation for them and this course did exactly that.

The goal of this book is to have you, the leader, walk away with a firm foundation so you don't have to learn the hard way.

When we talk about leadership, we hear the words *foundation* and *pillars*. Both give me the impression of solid, but also unmoving and intimidating buildings. In your leadership role you will be constantly learning and changing. The world changes so quickly now, and we need to change quickly too. As leaders we need to be like trees, solid in our roots but bending and shifting with the wind. My hope is that this book becomes like *roots* for you—giving you a solid foundation so you can sway with the wind but remain rooted in what's important to you and your company.

Root One: Know Yourself

When I ask people why they stepped into a leadership role, I often hear "It was the next logical step." I usually follow up with "Is it what you expected?" and the answer is always "No!" The reasons vary, but I've rarely heard anyone say, "It was exactly what I expected." The answer to "If you could go back, would you do it again?" varies. Most say, "Yes," but I think that has more to do with the fact that they are attending some form of leadership talk from me. If they were going to say no to that question, they probably would have already stepped out of the role.

To be an effective leader, we must know ourselves well. Leading a team means making tough decisions and supporting a group of people to get the work done. At times this can be overwhelming, and if we don't know ourselves well, it's going to be hard to make those tough choices. Not to mention keep ourselves in a good space in order to make those decisions.

If I asked you the question "Who are you?" you'd probably start your answer with your name. Depending on the context of the conversation, you might follow up with your family name or define yourself by someone I might know in your family; i.e., "I'm Jane Smith's daughter." If it's more of a work context, the follow up to your name is more likely to be your role or maybe your department.

If you want to really see people squirm, say, "Tell me about yourself" and provide zero context. Most people struggle with this because we rarely take the time to get to know ourselves, and we are very complex beings.

When we step into a leadership role, knowing ourselves becomes more important. The moment you become a leader your sphere of influence increases, as well as your responsibility. You are no longer taking care of a set of tasks; you are now responsible for the sets of tasks multiple people are responsible for. More responsibility and far less control. Getting a task done no longer requires knowledge of the task itself. Now you need to understand the inner working of the team member, what's going on in their lives, what their personality needs to get things done, what's happening with other team members that might be getting in the way of getting the task done, and so much more. I like the phrase "Being on the balcony" because you have to step back and take a view of the bigger picture, and you have to be aware of the whole picture. Sometimes it's exhausting watching how everything is fitting together (or worse, figuring out why it's not fitting).

In this section we will talk about getting to know ourselves in order to:

- Protect our energy
- Understand our own needs
- Understand our frustration and emotions
- Communicate our needs

Getting to know yourself is not a one and done. As we learn, grow, and age, our lives change and what we need to keep our personal energy up changes as well. Sometimes it's something happening in our lives, a major change, like moving, changing jobs, having a family, or losing members of our family. During those times, how we practice self-care and what we need to show up as our best selves changes. Sometimes those things are short-lived and other times they are things that happen in our lives that change things for a much longer period.

Then we will talk about understanding others, especially those that aren't like us, in order to:

- Understand their frustration and emotions
- Hear their needs
- Use our differences to come to the best solutions

Same can be said here, people need space to learn and grow. If we aren't a one and done, neither are they, so give them grace and see when they have improved in some area.

Last but not least, I'll share my favorite framework for understanding ourselves and others.

As a leader, your time is no longer spent "doing" the work; you are now ensuring that the work is done through others. In order to do this, you need a good understanding of yourself so you can also understand your team.

Chapter 1

Who Am I?

Ask a person this question "Who are you?" and watch how they struggle to answer. Such a short sentence, but it leaves people somewhat stuck. There are just too many ways to answer the question. Usually, they will ask for context first, and if you don't offer any, they will often start to give their job title, if they have children, who they are in relation to what they do or their surrounding relationships.

Try it for yourself. Who are you?

While this is an incredibly difficult question to answer, it's important that you understand yourself.

- What are your strengths?
- What are your weaknesses?
- What are your preferred methods of communication?
- How do you want people to communicate with you?
- How do you like to communicate with others?
- What are your triggers (those things that just frustrate you to no end)?
- Where are you hard on yourself?

When you step into a leadership role, you suddenly become responsible for yourself as well as the decisions of your entire team. That's a lot of responsibility. When I work with leaders, I often say, "Yes, that is your responsibility," or "You need to deal with that behavior immediately." The consequences of not dealing with issues are longer and more far-reaching than most leaders realize. In order to be aware of what's happening and be able to deal with it, you need to show up every day with the best energy you can muster. This means getting to know yourself so you know what you need in any given moment.

We all have four parts to our being:

- Physical – to move
- Mental – to think
- Spiritual – to connect
- Emotional – to feel

We need to understand these parts of ourselves and know how to deal with them when we are struggling with any of them. They are all connected, so struggling in one part will cause problems for the others. Most of us have a "go to" when we are struggling. I used to use the physical. When faced with any stress, I would exercise and get all the excess energy out. Others are more emotional, and when they experience stress, they might take a moment and yell or cry to move that energy.

The physical is usually the easy one for people to understand. It's about how we take care of our physical body, what we eat, when and how much we move, etc. Taking care of your physical body is not about a new workout trend or having the perfect physique, because that will cause problems in other areas if it's not your thing. You do need to move though, so do it in a way that you enjoy. Eat the foods that make you feel good.

Our mental energy is something that we don't think as much about, but just like our physical body we need to be aware of what we are "feeding" our minds. This has become more important with social media and algorithms. Social media shares with us the things it thinks we want to know about. When there is a controversy in our world, we are bombarded with it on social media, and it can start feeling overwhelming. Our minds also need more downtime than we give them. This is why I like baking so much. Mostly I only like baking things that I have done often so I don't have to focus too hard on it. It gives my brain some rest.

Spiritual energy is different for everyone. It's our ability to connect. For some that comes in the form of a religious belief system that requires they do things like pray to connect to a deity of their choice. For others it's a meditation and so on. Still there are those that don't connect with the idea of a deity or other spiritual being; each of them has their own way of connecting. I have a friend who doesn't believe in any of the spiritual stuff, but when I walk in the forest with her, I see more animals than I ever do alone. She will talk to them and take pictures. She connects with Nature. We all need a way to connect to something.

Emotional energy is the hardest for me. It's something I work on constantly. I am not a person who is highly aware of her emotions. My emotions control me more often than I wish they did. The same as all the others, though, we need to be aware of what we feed our emotions. Sometimes it's people in our lives who say hurtful things, but sometimes it's the thoughts in our own heads wreaking havoc. Either way, we need to be aware and decide what we let into our lives. The ability to name and control our emotions is the hardest for many people, because we weren't taught. It's worse for men in Western society, because they have been taught that it's only OK to show anger, but not too much that they lose control.

Protect Your Energy

Getting to know ourselves allows us to protect our own personal energy. We all have things that we enjoy doing, and then there are those parts of our lives and jobs that we do not enjoy but are necessary evils. If we are doing too many of those necessary evils, we will find our energy drained. If we ignore all those things, we will find ourselves in some form of difficulty because those parts NEED to be taken care of as well. Here are three suggestions:

1. *Sandwich tasks you don't enjoy with tasks you do enjoy.* Do them in smaller bits so that you aren't spending hours doing the pieces that you really don't enjoy. This will help you to maintain your energy throughout the day.

   An example for me is any task that requires me to sit still for long periods of time. Like writing this book! I usually write early in the morning or just before lunch so that my next activity is something that gives me energy. If it's early in the morning, my next activity is a walk with the dog. The dog is ecstatic to go, so it's always an enjoyable outing and it gets me moving. If I write just before lunch, I get to leave the office for an hour or so after, and I usually find a game or a funny show to watch over lunch, and the obvious, eating, again something I enjoy doing.

2. *Be kind to yourself (which always turns into more kindness for others).* Think of that task or thing that you struggle with. How often do you chastise yourself in your own mind for not staying on that task or for not doing a better job at it? Mine is staying organized. I'm great at taking a day to organize myself. I create beautiful spreadsheets, make binders, and create files (sometimes even color-coded), but then life gets busy, and I forget my whole system! The files are there, but the papers are everywhere. Then I have another day where I clean it all up and I realize I had a system, but I forgot about it. I now just laugh about it, but previously I had some choice words for myself in these situations. I promise you they were not kind words.

   My suggestion here is to be kind to yourself on these things and maybe get someone to help you with the areas that you struggle with. When I was in a management role with ten people reporting to me, we would have a ton of projects going on at once. As the leader, I could not keep all of it in my mind, so I used a spreadsheet. I was terrible at keeping the spreadsheet, so I had my assistant keep it updated for me. While not normally part of her role, she had a strength in organizing these types of things and was happy to take it on. Is there someone on your team that could take on some of the tasks that aren't your strengths?

3. *Be prepared.* I am fully aware that doing month-end financials is not my favorite thing, but it is necessary. I've gone back and forth on whether I should have someone take it over for me (I didn't have that option when I was in an HR managers position). The reality for me is that it's less than an hour a week, so I'd be hiring someone for ten minutes (because you know they would be so much faster than I am at it), plus I would still have to upload receipts etc. For now, the better business choice for me was to continue doing this work myself.

I can prepare myself for it, though, and use some of the tools I mentioned earlier like sandwiching. For me it looks like taking thirty minutes every Friday morning to put all the receipts in my system for the week. I update my spreadsheets and then end my week with something I enjoy. I am aware every week that this is what I'll be doing Friday morning, so I'm prepared for it, I know it's coming, and I do my best to keep things as organized through the week so that I'm not searching for things on Friday morning.

Know Your Values

Another important aspect of what you need to be aware of is your values. I shared in the introduction that I worked at a company that rocked my confidence. In reflecting on my time there, I realized that we had a very different set of values, and that values mismatch is what caused a lot of the issues.

My values are Strength, Drive, Integrity, Care for Others, and Vision. This company did not show care for others, the integrity was lacking, and there was no vision for our future. It was a long-standing company that felt like it wasn't going anywhere or trying anything new. Just the same old, same old. This did not match me at all. I was constantly battling with my boss and my management team and repeatedly told I was wrong and to "assimilate" to their way of doing things.

It was a difficult place to be. At every other company I'd worked at my work had been celebrated. To suddenly go from all that praise to being constantly told I was wrong didn't compute in my mind. I was in a constant state of stress and doing everything I could to deal with the stress. For me that looked like extreme workouts, which should have had me in great shape, but I constantly had illnesses that, when reviewed, medically were nothing. This is when the doctor told me to take a vacation or he'd put me on sick leave.

Contrast this to the company I mentioned in the opening. Their values were so close to mine that when I was in university and had to create a company's benefits package, mine was very close to theirs. This was a learning company; when they learned something new, they implemented it, they cared for their employees, and they were very clear on their vision and made it known to all of us. Working there, I had stress—not everything went right—but my team came together and worked out a solution. The vision and values for the company were so clear that we had great guidelines with which to make the decisions, and we knew if we met them, our decisions would be backed up. I still did extreme sports at the time, but it was just for fun; it wasn't required, and my health was so much better—no bizarre illnesses with no explanation.

If you are at a company that does not meet your values, move on as soon as you can. Nothing good will come of it. If you are in management and you have a team member that has a set of values that don't meet your company values, let them go. It will better serve them to find a place more suited to them, and it will be more beneficial to your team.

I mentioned in the intro to this section that getting to know yourself is not a one and done. Sometimes we have a stressor in our life that changes our behavior, sometimes they are short term, and sometimes they are longer term. I had an extreme version of this the year I started running this business full time; I had half my thyroid removed *by mistake*. I won't go much further into that part here, but I will share that this changed me forever. It's been over eight years, and I'm still not back to who I used to be.

Before the surgery, when things got too stressful, I'd work out. I loved extreme sports and did some pretty heavy workouts. Things like CrossFit and P90X, mountain biking on single-track trails, running half marathons (not my favorite, but I can say I did it once!), snowboarding, kayaking, scuba diving. Anything to get that rush of adrenaline and release all the stress from my job. After the surgery, I did not have the energy for the workouts. It's not that I couldn't do them; I could, but I'd burn out and have to spend the next two days on the couch.

I went from P90X and CrossFit to walking my dog (a fourteen-pound dog who only needs a fifteen-minute walk) and doing at the most ten minutes of exercise. I hate to admit that it took me way longer than it should have for me to figure out that this was going to be my life going forward. I tried for years to build myself back up to twenty or thirty minutes, but every time I did, I'd burn out again and it would take me a few days (or sometimes weeks) to recover. I no longer had exercise as a way to deal with my stress; even something seemingly easy, like yoga, I can still only do ten minutes. I had to learn new ways.

Western medicine felt that there was nothing wrong with me. My numbers were normal, but I was always exhausted. Thankfully I got help from naturopaths and a medical intuitive. I learned a new way to eat and accepted that ten minutes of exercise was going to have to be enough.

I have learned breathing techniques, meditation, mantras, and other techniques to use the other parts of my being to deal with the stress.

I also had to do some review of my values. Specifically, "Drive" . . . For me that always meant driving to a better physical version of me, and I did that through exercise and pushing my body to the limits. I could no longer do that anymore, so what did "Drive" even mean? I'm still driven, that hasn't changed, but now it's less in physical pursuits. I'm still always driving to be a better me, but now it looks like a better speaker, writer, and coach (also stepmom, girlfriend, daughter, sister, etc.).

To show up as the best version of ourselves, we have to know ourselves. That is a never-ending opportunity for learning. The more we grow and live, the more things will change. What we need this week is not necessarily what we need next week. Be patient with yourself. The more patience and understanding you have for yourself, the more you will have for others.

Chapter 2

Why Isn't Everyone Like Me?

In the last chapter we talked about getting to know yourself. Now I want you to think about the people in your life, especially the ones that drive you crazy. You know, the ones who don't behave like you. Maybe they are more laid back than you and not so rushed to get somewhere on time. Or maybe you are that person, and you are annoyed with the person who is always trying to rush you somewhere.

- With whom do you get along best?
- Who frustrates you the most?
- What parts of them frustrate you?
- What parts of them do you admire and wish you could do as well as they do?

Once we know and accept ourselves, it gets a lot easier to know and accept others. In Chapter 3 we'll walk through understanding different personalities. For this chapter I want you to see how celebrating our differences really helps you and your team.

Having a team allows you to share the tasks. Some you can even pass off to someone who has a strength that you do not. In my manager roles, I usually had an assistant. For the most part, those assistants were way better at keeping notes and spreadsheets on the teams' tasks. I would have them take care of it for me. The whole team would have access to the spreadsheet, and we would update our progress at meetings, but the assistant was the only one allowed to update the spreadsheet. I always enjoyed leading the meetings, but I wasn't so great at reminding everyone of what they promised. The team would agree on reminder timelines, and the assistant would send us reminders at whatever interval we had agreed on, but always twenty-four hours before the next meeting. This gave everyone time to be prepared for what they would have to update the following day.

It also allows you to model behavior. Early on in one of my roles I had a coach come in and do a DISC (Dominance, Influence, Conscientiousness, Steadiness) assessment with our team. The day was spent team building/getting to know yourself. DISC is a personality assessment that helps you understand yourself and gives your team the knowledge of how you like to be communicated with (more on this in the next chapter). Two interesting things came out of this day:

1. One of my employees expected me to be one personality and was surprised when I showed up as another personality. She felt I was more task-focused than people-focused. She shared this with a teammate. The teammate reminded her that if I was the personality she thought, then I would never have brought the team together for this type of training. The employee had seen me deal with a person with that personality and I had mirrored their communication style, making it look to her like that was my natural style.

2. That same staff member realized that I do not enjoy getting into the details and started to do her best to give me an abbreviated version of what I needed to know. When she had to share all the details, she would come to me and say, "You need to hear all the details—would you like them now, or after lunch?" She knew that sitting and listening to the

details would suck up all my energy, so she offered me the opportunity to listen now, or go and do something to bring up my energy at lunch, so I was ready to listen.

My staff member realized in the meeting that I was able to change my communication style to suit the person I was talking to when I needed to, and she also did her best to do the same for me. We were both able to be flexible enough to give the other what they needed. When we had a meeting where I knew that she would want more information and have more questions than I did, I would ask her to attend with me so that she would get all the information she needed and we would share with the rest of the team. Some would want all the information she requested and others, who were like me, just needed the high-level information. We used each other's strengths and accepted that we didn't share the same strengths.

That was a positive example of two people who could accept each other's strengths and weaknesses and work with them. I've also had situations that didn't start out quite so well.

In my first management job, very early on, I had a not-so-great conversation with a fellow management team member. I was sitting in my assistant's office with both of my direct reports. The health and safety manager came in and started telling me how to do my job, or at least that's what it sounded like to me. I said something to make it clear that this wasn't the time, but he didn't pick up on the subtle message and continued talking. I said it again in a much harsher tone, but he still didn't get it. The third time I made it *very clear* that he needed to leave the office immediately. My staff were both very uncomfortable but felt as I did, that he had come in to tell me how to do my job, and they got it the first time I said it and didn't understand why he kept talking.

There is another piece to this story that is important. This manager had been interviewed for the role I was hired for.

To his credit, he came to my office later when I was alone. I was still annoyed and not really ready to speak to him calmly.

Thankfully, we went ahead with the conversation anyway. I explained to him that coming in to tell me how to do my job in front of my team was inappropriate. I probably didn't say this in the kindest way because I was still annoyed. I was a young woman in a male-dominated organization, the first female to ever sit on the senior management team. It was already going to be an uphill battle. I didn't need him coming in and telling me how to do my job in front of my staff. He explained that that wasn't what he was doing. He finds joy in running through ideas and loves the process of discovering the best possible solution to a problem. His intention was to come and share ideas, hoping I would share my thoughts and punch holes in his ideas so we would come up with a better idea from both of our knowledge. I believe we also discussed the fact that he had applied for my job.

While this conversation was incredibly uncomfortable for both of us, it was the best thing that could have happened. We both left with a better understanding of each other, and since my human resources training taught me to train my replacement if I had plans to move up the corporate ladder, I told him I was happy to share my knowledge so that he was ready to take over when I left. We worked very well together after that. I taught him what I knew from a human resources perspective, and he helped me to better understand health and safety. While it was always difficult for me to have friends in an organization because of how little I could share with people, he and I have remained friends to this day, over sixteen years since that conversation and fourteen since I left the organization. Unfortunately, after working with me for about six months he decided that human resources was not for him, and he let me know that he no longer wanted to take over when I left. We found someone externally!

He and I never did a personality assessment together, but we were able to explain our likes and dislikes. We were also able to explain the situation we were in. It never occurred to him that being female might make my job harder, but he certainly understood after that conversation. This couldn't have happened if we hadn't both taken the time to get to know ourselves.

I'm incredibly grateful that we went forward with the conversation because I may not have been as honest if I'd calmed down first. What if we'd never had that conversation? Or if I'd calmed down and not been as open and honest with him? I imagine our working relationship would have been a very difficult one. Him thinking I was just an unkind person who wasn't willing to work through ideas with him, and me thinking he thought he knew more than I did about a position he never worked in. I imagine there would have been very little that would have changed our minds about each other.

That conversation allowed us to better understand each other and to change our initial judgments about each other. Think about that member of your team that you find difficult to work with. . . . Is there anything they can say or do to change your mind? Is there space for them to grow and change?

Having different personalities on a team is extremely helpful. When each team member brings their strengths to the table, it's so much easier to find the best possible solution because each team member will look at the situation from a different angle.

In one group of leaders that I've done a lot of work with, two of the leaders reported to the third leader, but they functioned very much as a team. Initially it was difficult because they had such different personalities. After attending the Leading with Ease course, which includes a personality assessment, they came to an understanding that their team was going to be high functioning because of their differences, but it was going to require a lot of communication.

Of the three, one was very people-focused, one could waver between people- and task-focus, and the third was incredibly task-focused and liked to get things done at a much faster speed than the other two. We had lots of conversations on how much of a strength this would be for the team. I know that they didn't find it easy. One of the things that they implemented after the course was a weekly management team meeting. They left the office and went to a local tea shop where they discussed what was going on in the team. They often disagreed on how to resolve issues, but because they understood one another, they were able to listen and come to a decision that they could all live with. They found a pace that felt slower for one and faster for the other two and always had a focus on both the people involved and the tasks that needed completing. Having three members on that management team with different personalities made everyone's life so much easier.

Recently they went through a major change. One of the team members had retired, and they let go of the weekly meetings, thinking that since it's just the two of them, they were no longer needed. It became clear that those meetings were still required. The minute they put them back in place, things got easier again.

While having different personalities at the table does make for better decision making, it also requires more communication. I saw this repetitively through the pandemic. I was called in for more mediations in two years than I had done in the seven years since I started my business. From a high level, most of the issues were miscommunication. People working from home and going into the office on opposite days didn't see one another for months at a time. Because they all had different styles, this left everyone to create stories in their head about why someone was doing things a certain way. When we got them together to mediate a discussion, they remembered the things they liked about one another and were able to work together again.

Not everyone is like you; not everyone is like me. That is a positive *if* we can take the time to understand one another and allow everyone to work with their strengths.

Chapter 3

DISC

The study of personality goes back years, right back to 400 BC, when Hippocrates (the doctor's oath is named after him: Hippocratic Oath) came up with four personalities. The personalities were grouped as sanguine, melancholic, phlegmatic, and choleric. Don't look up the meaning of those words—they are all fluids from the body!

Since then, there have been many different scholars who have done studies and come up with their own way to separate personalities, types, or communication styles: Jung, Myers-Briggs, Keirsey and Bates, Lowry, and Marston to name a few. They each shared their own way to categorize and understand different personalities.

In this book we will focus on the DISC theory created by William Marston in the 1920s. The way the test is done has changed over time, but the personality categories have remained the same. I find it helpful for leaders. The test results show you how to communicate with each style and where your strengths and weaknesses lie and where they might rub your teammates the wrong way.

When I do this process with groups, each person on the team takes the test and then we meet to discuss the results and how the team could better work together. With one particular group, one member told me right at the beginning of the meeting that she felt this was going to be a waste of time. I laughed and told her I'd win her over, and I did. I also thanked her for showing up as her personality; she was giving a great example of that style. After the session she had a much better understanding of her team and her leader. She was able to understand why they didn't work the way she did and why sometimes she got frustrated with the way they were doing things. She also understood that their strengths were a relief to her; she knew she had people who would naturally think differently than her and would be there to support her in her decision making.

It's important to note that no matter which personality assessment you take, any of the styles can be an effective leader, and no style is better than another. Each style is equally valuable and understanding that makes us a much better team.

Just because we have a particular spot on the circle doesn't mean we can't stretch and display the strengths of another personality. DISC is simply sharing where we are most comfortable. To be successful as a team, we need to be able to shift our style sometimes. It's important that one person isn't required to shift all the time, or they will be constantly exhausted.

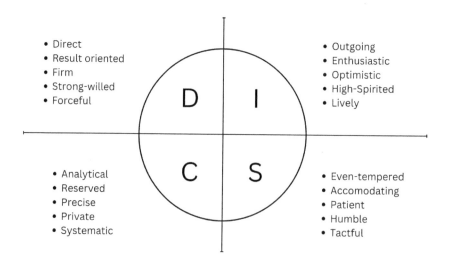

- Direct
- Result oriented
- Firm
- Strong-willed
- Forceful

D

- Outgoing
- Enthusiastic
- Optimistic
- High-Spirited
- Lively

I

- Analytical
- Reserved
- Precise
- Private
- Systematic

C

S

- Even-tempered
- Accomodating
- Patient
- Humble
- Tactful

For the purpose of this book, we will refer to each style by their letters. Sometimes people get hung up on the word. Women haven't exactly been celebrated for being "Dominant," though that word does suit the personality well. So, we will just use "D," "I," "S," and "C."

D style:

People with the D style are eager, they love a lofty goal, and they motivate themselves. They are ready to take on the tasks assigned to them; they might even create their own tasks if the leader isn't giving them enough to do. They voice their opinions easily. They are internally motivated and rarely need to be encouraged. They can be questioning and skeptical but are willing to take risks to get the results they want. They will constantly be looking for new and exciting projects.

I style:

You can spot an I style easily; they are usually upbeat and optimistic. They are incredibly social, have a very expressive nature, and love to be the center of attention. They want a fun and collaborative work environment. They want to work with others and love to make personal connections. They love a good conversation and will bring up discussion just to talk about interesting things, and not necessarily stay on task. They love to improvise and make spontaneous decisions.

S style:

The S style is all about heart. If you want to know what's going on in your team, your S style has already checked in with anyone who might have shown any signs of stress. They like a friendly and collaborative environment (like the I style) but prefer to focus on their tasks without being interrupted. They need time to adapt to change and want to be recognized for their efforts (but not necessarily publicly). It's important to an S to know they are making a difference on the team.

C style:

C style are the people who will eventually come up with a way to "beam" us up to space. Their favorite question is "Why not?" They focus on facts and logic and strive for quality results. They are comfortable working alone and love to analyse concepts and examine solutions. They will consider all consequences before choosing an action. Like S styles, they prefer to have lots of time to deal with a change; they need the time to consider every part of a change.

I used to write letters to my team at the end of the year, thanking them for their work. I was specific about particular things they had done well.

- The S styles were so touched by the effort.
- The I styles were more excited about the team lunch where they received the letter.
- The C styles were happy if the letter was more specific about how they brought their expertise and avoided the "feelings" stuff.
- My D style employee said to me, "I don't need this." He didn't, but I gave him one every year anyway!

Where You Fit on the Circle

DISC places the styles in a circle. This is helpful for several reasons.

1. It shows where each style meets.
   a. At the top of the circle, D and I meet in speed; they prefer to do things quickly.

   b. The bottom of the circle has S and C meeting for the same reason, but they prefer a moderate pace; they need time to adjust.

   c. On the left, D and C meet in their focus on task.

   d. On the right, I and S meet in their focus on people.

2. It shows which styles might clash the most.

   a. D and S do things very differently. D is task-focused and quick to make decisions. S styles are people-focused and like a moderate pace.

   b. C and I also have a very different style. I is people-focused and fast, and C is task-focused and prefers a moderate pace.

3. It helps us manage our personal energy. When you do the test, they place a dot where you would fit in the circle. If you think of that dot as a pin with an elastic around it, every time you are asked to work in another style, think of that elastic being stretched. The energy it's taking you is the same as the energy to pull the elastic. In a style that's close to yours, it might not take too much energy but being pulled all the way across the circle will suck up your energy.

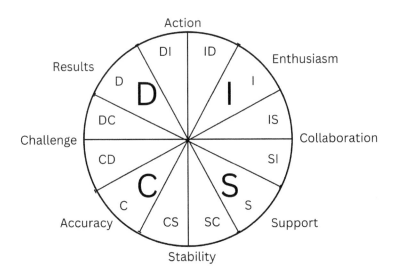

If you haven't guessed yet, I'm a DI. I can move easily between the D and the I, but when I'm asked to pay particular attention to detail or work too long by myself, I need to do something that will bring my energy back. Writing this book happened in small increments, with lots of exercise/stretching or social activity between writing sessions.

So far, we discussed the direct styles. Each person is unique in that they fit somewhere on this circle and sometimes are very close to being in two styles. The image in the previous page shows how you could have two letters as your style. As I mentioned, I'm a DI style. If you look around the circle in the image, you will see the main priority of each style, including the hybrids. For example, as a DI, I prioritize action, the CSs or SCs are focused on stability, and so on.

How We Communicate

Each style has a preference in the way that they communicate. Below are some quick tips on how to communicate with each style.

D style:

They are quick and like communication that is quick and to the point. It's important to stay on topic and eliminate time wasters.

Be bright, be bold, be gone!

I style:

They prefer to be approached informally and love to laugh. Keep the conversation light. They need space to verbalize their thoughts and feelings, remember that they are processing so it's not necessarily their final thoughts and feelings.

Be attentive, be inspiring, be positive!

S style:

While S style is all heart, they need space. Respect their personal space and property. Be clear and specific, but soft in your approach. Sincerity is important. If you don't believe what you are saying, they will know it from a mile away. They have a very sensitive "baloney" detector.

Be kind, be specific, be quiet!

C style:

Dependability is very important to a C. They prefer precise, tactful, and emotionally reserved conversations and will want you to remain focused on the task.

Be knowledgeable, be focused, be prepared!

When we aren't feeling good

In 2020 and 2021 it became more important than ever for me to share what happens when each style is "out of esteem." This refers to all the negative emotions that take over from time to time: sadness, stress, overwhelm, etc. The entire world was dealing with a pandemic and our emotions were running high. We all had lockdowns, rules that changed daily, huge changes in the way we worked and lived. Everyone was dealing not only with the pandemic but with their own personal reality within the pandemic. I think it's safe to say that most of us were "out of esteem."

D style:

When the D style is "out of esteem," they can become intolerant and impatient. They may pull away from social interaction and become bored and restless. Their demeanor might seem more aggressive and insensitive.

I style:

When "out of esteem," the I style may exaggerate and become unreliable or scattered. They may have a much stronger need to be the center of attention and consequently may take on too much. At the same time, they can become more sensitive and easily hurt.

S style:

The S style may also take on too much because they will start to people-please and be unable to say no. Then they may have difficulty identifying priorities and meeting deadlines. They will look for constant praise and will avoid conflict at all costs.

C style:

"Out of esteem," the C style will become overly concerned with perfection, while hampering creativity with rules. They will seem pessimistic and, like S, will resist change. Like D, they may isolate themselves or become mistrusting of the team.

It's important to be aware of your own tendencies as well as those of your team. When you start to see the behavior in someone else, you will know to ask questions or give them some space. You can also ask your team to let you know when you are showing any of the above behaviors so that you can do what you need to get yourself back in a better space.

There are many different personality, style, and communication assessments. This one is my preference, but I know others who feel that another one is more suited to them. Whichever you choose, keep it close. Having the information is not helpful if we don't use it in our day-to-day. When we use it in our day-to-day, each member of the team feels celebrated for their unique strengths, which turns into better communication, better decision making, and better profits. (For those working in nonprofit, it turns into more people helped by your work.)

Root Two: Know the Destination

Another important aspect of leading is knowing where you are headed, how you plan to get there, and what values your team should share in getting you there. The clearer you are on all three, the easier it is to make decisions. At any crossroads you can go back to your vision, mission, and values, and then choose the action that most matches all three. If you are clear on this, you will define your company culture instead of it defining you.

Company culture is the beliefs and behaviors that determine how a company's employees and management interact. It's the sum of your formal and informal systems, behaviors, and values, all of which create an experience for your employees and customers. Culture is passed on in several ways, sometimes by formal systems, written instructions, etc., but it can also be passed by stories. If the stories that your staff are sharing are not in line with the culture that you are aiming for, a culture you didn't plan will be created.

Vision, mission, and values will each have their own chapter, but it is important that all three work together. We have all had the experience when a company says they are the friendliest place to be, and then we see a staff member being mistreated by the supervisor. If you are not friendly to your own staff, no one will believe that you are the friendliest place to be.

When creating your vision, mission, and values, they should inform each other. For example, if part of your vision or mission is to have the best products, then you might have a value for innovation. How will you have the best products if you aren't innovating all the time? This can lead to more questions as well. How will you have innovation if your staff aren't comfortable sharing their ideas? Maybe then you also need a value of respect or idea flow. Curiosity is your friend here. Just keep asking, "What do we need to ensure _____?" Fill in the blank at each step.

When I think of all three working together, I picture our vision as a scene at the end of a long road, our mission is the road we are on and how we are currently traveling that road, and our values are the guideposts keeping us on the road. All three need to be working together so that we are staying on the road with the vision always in sight. I like to picture the guardrails far apart so that we have lots of room for creativity but remain true to who we want to be.

If you prefer the tree analogy, your vision is the sun that we are all growing toward.

For this section I will focus on two companies that have created a strong vision, mission, and values, and worked hard to ensure that they were living and breathing documents as opposed to words written on a wall. Both companies have been incredibly successful. Both are international and both have been, at one point or another, voted as one of the best companies to work for. I was uncomfortable using companies that everyone might know, because I didn't work there and feel the difference myself. One of the companies I actually worked for, and the other I have experienced through Toastmasters. They have a corporate club that I have been able to visit on multiple occasions, and a close friend previously worked for them. Their previous president and founder also agreed to speak with me to explain how they got to where they are now. I trust when I'm sharing the stories for these two companies that they are what they say they are.

I mentioned in Root One the difference between working at a company with values that matched mine and what happened when I worked for a company where our values did not match. You might wonder how the latter happened. It happened because the people interviewing me misrepresented themselves in the interview. When I was providing examples of how I'd used the innovation I'd seen in different companies to better the HR teams in subsequent companies I'd worked at, their response was "That's great, we need someone with new ideas." However, their reality was not that. When I would suggest new ideas or share how we'd done something differently, they would simply say, "Assimilate, Lisa." Perhaps it was something that particular manager wanted them to be, but it was not who they were.

The clearer you are with your vision, mission, and values, the easier it is for you and your team. Everyone will be headed toward the same vision and using the values as the guidepost to make decisions. This will allow you to create the culture that you want instead of having a culture created for you. You will also attract people who want to help you. Those who don't will move on (whether asked to or by their own choice). It would have been great if that company had been clear with me about who they were. I could have avoided working there at all.

It does not stop there, though; it will be your responsibility as the leader to ensure that everyone is working within the framework. If they are, find a way to celebrate them and share with the team. If they aren't, you need to take action to get them back on track. While it is wonderful to be clear on where you are headed and how you want to get there, if you are not actioning those beliefs every day, people will start to see through your words and will stop believing you, but more on that in Root Three.

Chapter 4

What Is the Final Destination?

Clients often come to me complaining about how difficult it is to keep their staff motivated. When I ask about their vision, I usually get a blank stare. It's no longer enough to hire someone to put together a part. They want to know why they are putting that part together. They want to feel like they are contributing to the world in some way. When you are clear on your vision, even the lesser parts of the business are bearable for everyone.

Recently I was listening to a friend speak about her experience working for a company where she dealt with sexism. The story was from the 1970s. Not only did she deal with sexism, but the company also did not have very good safety practices. (We've come a long way on both since the time of her story.) While she was telling us all these negative things about the organization and how dangerous it was, she also mentioned the one product that they were known for. They were the best at creating this product, and it was sold all over the world. You could still see her pride in having been a part of that. While being proud of a particular product isn't necessarily a vision, that company had something that the team was proud to be a part of. It was their "scene" at the end of the road that they all worked to ensure.

When we are clear about where we are going, our team will be motivated by that future state and will work through the difficult pieces of the job to continue helping to work toward that vision. They might see the improvements that have been made toward it but know that there is always more road to travel. The statement itself keeps them motivated to consistently do better and learn more.

I googled the definition of *vision,* and the second definition fit my understanding: "the ability to think about or plan the future with imagination or wisdom."

When creating your vision, it needs to be something far enough away that you can continue striving for it. You want the statement to inspire your team to keep working toward it. It's not a goal, it's an end state. It can be written in a way that you will never get there, like IKEA's "create a better everyday life for many people." That will never be finished; we will constantly learn more and continue to make things "better," so it is a constantly moving target but keeps our eyes on a better future.

The best company I ever worked for was Magna International. Their mission statement now reads:

Creating a better world of mobility, responsibly.

This is not something I remember from working there (and at the time it may have been a different statement), but it is what I was working toward when I was there. The statement that always stuck in my mind was "better product at a better price" (more on that in the third part of this root). That meant we were always innovating, trying to decrease the cost of making each part, and finding the most innovative product and ways to create those products. It was always clear to me that we were to service the community, planet, and our people.

While I haven't worked at Cementation, their previous president, Roy Slack, shared how he created his vision, mission, and values. Cementation's founding vision statement is:

To fundamentally change the way mine contracting is carried out within our industry, for the benefit of all stakeholders.

When you look at both Magna's and Cementation's vision statements, they are things that will never be complete. In Magna's "Creating a better world of mobility, responsibly" you will never "arrive" at that. We will as a society continue to learn more about mobility, and Magna will continue to make things better with the work they are doing. Cementation's vision statement will also never be complete. They have made huge strides in changing the way mine contracting is carried out, but there will always be more to do.

You will also note Magna use the term *mobility*; they are an automotive (read car) parts manufacturer. They use the term *mobility* because it leaves them room to grow into many different areas of mobility. Cementation is clearer about their definition. They are mine contractors and have no intention of moving out of that particular area at this point. If they decide to, they will have to reimagine their vision statement.

The statement itself is important, but if you are not making decisions that support the vision, people will lose faith. For an extreme example, let's use Cementation's last phrase, "for the benefit of all stakeholders." As an employee, if you read that and then find out that the company is doing something that harms the environment, you are not going to feel very motivated to create that vision. People that live near those mine projects are also stakeholders. Same result if you see a manager yelling at an employee—employees are also stakeholders, and no one wants to be yelled at.

The vision needs to be inspiring:

- It should *paint a picture* of a future state that your team will be motivated to work toward.
- It should be a *short* sentence that is easy to remember; many websites suggest two sentences at the most.
- Be *specific*; focus on what you do as an organization. Like Magna, you can leave room for growth by using a term like *mobility*; it's broader but allows more space to grow in the future.
- Avoid using technical jargon. It should be stated *simply* so that your team and anyone outside the company understands it. Your vision will attract both clients and future employees. Society is now focused more on wanting meaning in their work and the companies they support.
- As mentioned in the introduction, it needs to be *aligned* with your mission and values.

Just having the vision is not enough. Because they are short sentences that are easy to remember, you need to make sure that there are some other parts that will ensure understanding. That is where we get to mission and values.

Chapter 5

How Are We Getting There?

You have the vision—the scene at the end of the road. Often the vision statement is a very short statement that is easy for people to remember. We used the examples of Magna and Cementation. Both are short, clear statements but left on their own could be misinterpreted. If you remember that picture of the vision being the scene at the end of a long road, the next step is to add a mission statement—the road itself and the way we will travel that road.

The best way to think about a mission statement is to think about a military mission: a group of people going to do a specific thing for a specific group of people. What road will you be traveling and how will you travel it?

To continue with our two examples:

Magna's mission, while they don't actually call it a mission statement, fits the mold:

> **We see a future where everyone can live and move without limitations. That's why we are developing technologies, systems, and concepts that make vehicles safer and cleaner, while serving our communities, the planet and, above all, people. Forward. For all.**

Cementation's founding mission:

> **To earn the distinction of being the mining contractor of choice of both client and employees through excellence in safety, performance beyond all expectations, and building of long-term relationships based on a "best for project" philosophy.**

Both mission statements help to clarify the visions we read in the last chapter. As a reminder, Magna's vision is "Creating a better world of mobility, responsibly." Cementation's is "To fundamentally change the way mine contracting is carried out within our industry, for the benefit of all stakeholders." Both missions help to clarify the visions, to give them more context and clarity on who they plan to serve and how they will serve them. They both reference safety, their stakeholders, and how they will perform.

You can see as an employee how, with both statements in place, it starts to get easier to make decisions. If you are at a crossroads and struggling to make decisions, you can look at the vision and mission to gain clarity. Let's use the example of how to handle waste from both companies.

There are three ways to handle waste:

1. The *proper* ways to handle waste (the best-known way at this time)
2. The *less than proper but still legal* ways to handle waste (still safe but not the best way)
3. The *fully illegal and damaging* ways to handle waste (obviously this one harms many)

Between their vision and mission statements, both companies have made it clear that they would expect their employees to choose #1, the *proper* way. Both state that they are concerned with communities in either their vision or their mission statements.

Neither would support anything less than what we know now as the best way to handle it. They also have statements that there would be an expectation that you are continuing to learn better ways to handle the waste, or even better yet, better ways to reduce the waste. Magna states, "developing technologies, systems, and concepts" and Cementation states, "performance beyond all expectations" and "best for project." As an employee at either company, it is clear that you are to choose the best way for multiple reasons, while continuing to strive to do better as you learn more.

Companies that don't provide this clarity leave the vision open to interpretation. While both Magna and Cementation have done a great job on their vision statements, staff could interpret "responsibly" in the case of Magna to mean being responsible solely to the shareholder, which they could interpret to mean "make the most money possible." In the case of Cementation, without the clarity, staff might not include the environment as a consideration, because they may not see the community at large as part of the stakeholders. Or maybe the placement of the mine, often far away from populated areas, would not warrant concern for the environment in their eyes.

A good mission statement describes the organization's purpose and how it serves its clients (and its staff) through its products or services.

It should answer:

- Who are your customers/clients?
- Why do you do what you do?
- What are the reasons or passions behind what you do?

The statement should be:

- *Inspirational*—like the vision, you want it to inspire both your staff and your customers.

- *Simple*—avoid the use of technical jargon. Use clear and simple language.
- *Be plausible and attainable*—our vision gives us the future's state. The mission should be something that we can actually "do."
- *Longer*—the mission can be a little longer than the vision. You need it to clarify some things. While still simple and concise, it can be more than two sentences.
- *Reference some values*—the values need to be written out separately, but your mission statement can reference the most important aspects of them.

The vision keeps that far-off picture in our minds, and the mission brings us clarity on the road to take and how we plan to travel that road. Next, we must put up the guideposts to make sure everyone stays safely on that road.

Chapter 6

What Is Important?

We now have the scene at the end of the long road. We know what road we are traveling on and how we will travel it. Now we need to put up the guideposts. These keep everyone on the road working in the same direction in the same way. It helps to clarify even further the expectations of everyone working there. I like to picture these guideposts as being far apart. While we want people to be clear on our values, we also want them to have room for creativity and innovation. Our world changes too quickly to stifle creativity and innovation.

Magna did this incredibly well. They have something called the employee charter; it was loosely based on the Magna Carta. It sets out a "blueprint for fairness" and makes it very clear for all employees and managers. The principles set out have been used in many countries and cultures. They worked to create something that was as universal as it could be.

Their principles are as follows:

- Job Security
- Competitive Wages and Benefits
- A Safe and Healthful Workplace
- Fair Treatment
- Employee Equity and Profit Participation

- Communication and Information
- The Hotline (this isn't a principle, but more a way to get help if you feel your team isn't meeting the above)

For instance, under job security, the explanation is "Being competitive by making a better product at a better price is the best way to enhance job security." I left this company seventeen years ago, so you know that it was important if I still remember it. I couldn't have recited it verbatim, but I remembered the sentiment.

Magna didn't just put these principles on the wall. They lived and breathed them. I can't say they were perfect. They are a huge international company, and no one can control everything perfectly. I can tell you that I have run into other people who have worked there, and while they too had left for various reasons, they still feel very positive about Magna as a whole.

It was made very clear to me when I started that these principles were important. Our employee handbook was separated by the six principles. The files in my office were organized based on the principles, and the principles were posted *everywhere!* I personally did extensive training on them because I was in human resources and was put through six months of what they called "Human Resources University," a collection of management training for the HR professionals that worked for Magna. They had the same type of training for their general managers. While I was there, they were creating the same type of course for all the supervisors across the company.

Cementation also has a set of values:

Our corporate values remain unchanged regardless of strategy, client, geographical location of work, or other dynamic factors within our business.

- Our belief in working safely and eliminating injuries must pervade everything we do. We are committed to safety because it is the right way to work.

- We want to treat our people well and give them every opportunity to succeed within our business and in life.
- We want to establish and maintain long-term relationships with clients, suppliers, and partners.
- We must be honest with our clients and base project decisions on what is best for the project.
- We want to be proud of the projects we carry out.
- We strive to work as a team within our own group, with our parent company and sister companies and with our clients, suppliers, and partners.
- We cannot be afraid to try new ideas that do not compromise safety.
- We must be performance driven on our projects, in our head office, wherever we apply ourselves. This ultimately means results-driven and action-based.

Although I personally never worked for Cementation, one of my friends did, and he assures me that these values were being lived and breathed as well. The former president and founder talked to me about how important it was to him that the values were felt "at the face." This is a term in mining that references the employees at the front lines of the business. "The face" is where the ground will be broken to find the needed ore. It was important to them that these weren't just words on the page at head office. They wanted to ensure everyone throughout the company knew, felt, and lived these values.

I have also worked for companies that put the values on the wall but do not live them. I won't mention names here, but one in particular had a value statement about treating everyone with dignity and respect, but they didn't hold anyone accountable to that. In that organization I was working with a union steward who was well known to be a bully. Shortly after I arrived, he would shout at me or insult me or other members of the management team. I tried talking to him, I tried setting boundaries, I tried leaving the room or a call when he was behaving inappropriately, and nothing changed. As a human resources professional, I felt that this employee should be disciplined for this behavior. I was warned not to do it without the explicit permission of my boss. When I spoke to my boss about it, I was told, "That's just (insert name)." I pointed out that this behavior was prohibited according to their values and that I felt it was our role as managers to ensure that the values were upheld. I was met with "Do NOT discipline this employee," with no explanation.

I did not feel this was right, but there was little I could do other than to keep myself out of harm's way, so I stopped speaking to him. We had another steward attend meetings where possible, and I kept other interactions short.

Unlike at Magna, when you speak to people who have left this company, they do not speak highly of their time there; most are relieved to have left. They were paid well, and that's all they can say as a good thing. They had a very high percentage of employees doing other work, either for their own small business or for another business. I had personally never seen numbers that high. I too started my coaching business while working there. I needed something that I could believe in.

It's not only important to write out your values, but you need to live them every day. Having a value of respect and doing nothing while someone yells insults at people is not living your values, and people know that. It breeds other poor behavior and disloyalty. On the other hand, having a value of respect and dealing with the staff who are showing disrespectful behavior will breed loyalty, and people will be way more willing to work hard for you.

After Cementation had created their vison, mission, and values, they did everything they could to share the successes in areas where they had followed their culture. One such example was a project they were working on where they ran into weak and fractured rock while sinking a mine shaft. (A mine shaft is a large diameter hole, often 1,000 or more meters deep, that is excavated through solid rock and is used to transport workers in and out of the mine and to bring ore out of the mine. Think of the tunnel an elevator passes through, but the walls are dirt and the elevator takes you deep into the earth.) There were two possible ways to support this weak rock, and both would have been effective. One way would have been more costly to the mine owner and result in larger profits for Cementation, and one would have been less costly to the owner and resulted in less profit for Cementation. Cementation recommended the less costly (less profit to them) approach because they felt it was best for the project.

Magna had many stories like this as well. While the "communication and information" principle was written so that employees had access to information about how the business was doing, the lines of communication went both ways. Remember that innovation was important at Magna. An employee working on a line came up with the idea that running boards on a truck did not have to stick out, they could tuck in under the truck and come out when the doors open. This idea was put forward and actually ended up as an option on a half-ton truck, even though Magna did not manufacture trucks, just their parts. This employee's idea was created and sold! He wasn't an engineer or manager. He worked on the line making parts and his idea was taken, and he received help from the engineers and managers to make sure that the idea made it to market. Even better, that story was shared with the whole company.

It's important to have your vision, mission, and values, but like anything else, you must sell it. Both companies used every opportunity they had to share stories about successes. Not monetary successes but the success of their vision, mission, and values in action. Keeping employees motivated is a lot like marketing—you have to remember to share all the great things that are happening that are moving the team closer to the vision.

Root Three: Know Your Role

In Brene Brown's book *Dare to Lead,* she mentions that as part of her research on leadership she discovered that when someone initially steps into the leadership role, they are no longer sure of how they add value to the company.[1] I was so excited to hear this because it explained so much of what I was seeing in my coaching business and what I'd personally experienced when stepping into my first leadership role.

When I'm coaching a leader, half of what I do is give them permission to do things. The instinct is there, but there is all this uncertainty. There is also a feeling that they aren't doing enough. I remember that feeling. I spent my day in meetings, talking to people, looking at projects or getting updates on them, but there was nothing tangible that I could say I did at the end of the day. No product, spreadsheet, or document that I could show someone that I had completed. Nothing! This makes you feel like you haven't done anything even though you were busy all day.

But you have! Your role as a leader is no longer being the "doer"; you are now coordinating what needs doing, and that takes a lot more time than you think. It involves being aware of all the projects on the team that reports to you as well as the management

---

[1] Brene Brown, *Dare to Lead: Brave Work, Tough Conversations, Whole Hearts* (New York: Random House, 2018).

team you are now a part of. The company as a whole needs to be working toward the same goals, and you need to be aware of how your part in the process affects others in the business.

We have all heard of the "natural" confrontations in businesses:

- Maintenance needs the time to fix machinery when production is fighting to keep the equipment running all the time.
- Sales makes promises that development can't back up.
- Sales and marketing also have a historical conflict.

When the leaders on both teams are working together, there are no "natural" confrontations, only discussions about what each team needs until they come to a decision that is best for the company as a whole. Think of Cementation's "best for project" philosophy.

We discussed in Root Two the importance of culture. Mission, vision, and values are part of creating the culture, but they mean nothing if the leaders are not ensuring that everyone is working within those parameters. As a leader, *you are the keeper of the culture.* If someone is working outside of the expectations, it is your job to deal with it. How to deal with it depends on the situation, and in my experience every situation requires a different approach. There are way too many factors to be able to give you a checklist or a decision tree; as a leader you will have to make the hard decisions and have the difficult conversations (that's Root Four).

That can sound ominous and leave you feeling like you only ever get to deal with things when something goes wrong. While that is the case, it's also important to celebrate the wins, as well as share the stories of when things went well, or someone did something that matched the business values so well. That is also part of keeping your culture and is equally important. While much of the coaching I do with leaders is helping them get comfortable with confronting behaviors when things aren't going right, we also have to have an equal amount of focus on celebrating every part of the journey so that we have practice when it's time for the big celebration.

We all have a choice in how we react to things. As leaders we also have a responsibility to create a team culture where others aren't afraid to come forward with decisions they made or let us know when they made a mistake. The more comfortable the environment you create, the better functioning team you will have.

Chapter 7

What Is My Role Now?

In my first management role, I worked with a company that was trying to create a culture change (full story in chapter 13). I was blessed to be part of the team that worked on the initial project. One of the first things that we did was come up with a definition of leadership, and I follow it to this day. It was:

> Model, Teach, Create, and Develop Commitment to Personal Responsibility.

A very short sentence for a very big role. Your role is to show up with your own personal responsibility intact and model, teach, create, and develop a team commitment to it.

This is not as easy as it sounds. Let's dive into each part of that statement.

Personal responsibility means controlling what you can control and understanding how your decisions are affecting the world around you. It requires that you take full accountability for your actions, decisions, thoughts, and more.

Model: As a leader we need to *model* this behavior. While it might sound easy, it's not. It's affected by so many things. Our mood, how tired we are, what's happening in our lives outside of work, how stressed we are, if we are hungry . . . and so on. That means as leaders we have to pay attention to each of these aspects of ourselves so when we are dealing with something, we still show up in the best way we possibly can.

I want to be clear: This does not mean you have to be perfect. It does mean that you must be clear about your own capabilities in every situation, and sometimes just be honest about it. It's OK to say, "I'm sorry, I can't help you right now; I'm dealing with something. Can we meet in the morning?" or to be honest with your team, "I'm struggling today; what do you need from me today and what can wait until tomorrow (or next week)?"

Teach: Once we are able to do this for ourselves, we *teach* those around us, both by our example and by being clear about our expectations. Being clear on our expectation doesn't stop there. If someone isn't meeting the expectation it is our responsibility to deal with it, that could mean a simple reminder, but it could also mean consequences, like disciplinary action.

Create: *Create* is a little different. This is less about the people and more about the environment, but it is still affected by our actions. We want to create an environment where it's safe for our teams to make mistakes. If we aren't creating a safe space, people won't want to tell us when they have made a mistake or when their project didn't go as planned. The safer the space, the more likely you will get all the information you need to make better decisions. Because it's more about the environment, sometimes it's harder to see. Examples are little things like someone rolling their eyes when another member of the team has an idea or wants to ask a lot of questions or telling someone that your door is always open but when they get there you bark at them and rush them through the questions they are trying to ask. Both are subtle but important in creating that safe space.

Develop: Last, but not least is *develop*. This is the all-encompassing word. If you have modeled, taught, and created, develop will follow. The actions in develop are the same as the other three. We work on ourselves as well as our team to make sure that we all have that commitment to personal responsibility.

The idea is that if each member of our team is personally responsible, we can work toward mutual accountability. This means that each member of the team agrees to be responsible for the commitments that they have voluntarily made to one another.

Life happens! So being committed doesn't mean exhausting ourselves to meet a deadline that is no longer feasible. It means that we go back to the person we made the promise to and renegotiate the deadline, or define which parts are still needed for that deadline.

In my current business, this happens at times. I will tell you it's far easier to do in a team than with a client. I was working on some job descriptions for a company I'd worked with regularly. I had given him a timeline and then had another client come in with a timeline that had larger consequences if I missed it. I called the first client to let him know what was happening and that I'd have to delay the deadline. He understood, and we agreed to a new date that worked for both of us. It really is that simple, but our minds make it so much harder than it needs to be.

While that paragraph is short and sweet, what went on in my head took a little longer. I did not want to disappoint this client because I have so much respect for him. I went through my calendar trying to find time to finish the job in our agreed upon timeline, but there was no extra time in my calendar that week. The next issue was if I tried to fit it in, I wouldn't do a good job of it and that makes me more uncomfortable than being late. I looked at every possible opportunity, letting go of family commitments, volunteer commitments, etc. There was no space in that week that I could step out of. In the end, the decision was to renegotiate the timeline, which the client was fine with; he wasn't in a rush. This process in my mind also took way longer than what it took to write this paragraph.

This is the role of a manager—we need to be able to see all parts of the situation. If there were any slight differences in the scenario, I would have made a different decision. If there was a rush for the job descriptions for some reason, I'd have found a way to do it. Maybe doing the work but having someone review it before I sent it out.

The example I like to give when working with leaders is that of two employees who have arrived late for work. The first employee has never been late and has worked for us for thirty years. The second is still in their probation period and has been late multiple times. Even though they were both late, they will be treated very differently. The first may simply be asked, "Is everything OK?" because this is so far out of their norm, while the second may be immediately terminated because they have shown themselves to be unreliable.

Or maybe employee one works a job where they are the only one in the role and they aren't held to a timeline. Their work is desk-type work and arriving late only forces them to do more work in less time that day, or they have to stay late to complete their tasks. But the second has held up an entire team from getting anything done in that time. Again, they will be treated very differently. The latter having created a larger consequence will likely receive a larger consequence.

We talked in the first root about knowing ourselves. This is where that becomes more and more important. If you know you are the type of person to react harshly, then know that when someone is late and you are annoyed, this isn't the time to have the conversation. Find time to calm yourself first so that you have time to review the entire situation. You don't want to be yelling at the thirty-year employee when they were only late once in thirty years. If you know you are the type of person to avoid confrontation, then do what you need to prepare to discuss the issue.

You are the keeper of the culture, and your team will be affected by how you have reacted to the situation. You do not want the rest of the team to see you being unreasonable with someone, but you also do not want them to think you are letting one team member get away with not doing their work/keeping up with the team.

It's also important to share when someone does something well. That employee that was late multiple times finally shows up on time for several weeks or months, let them know you are noticing the behavior. Also see "Joe the Supervisor" in chapter 14 to see how easy this can be.

Next, we consider some best practices for what you can and cannot say.

Chapter 8

Am I Allowed to Say That?

As a human resources manager, as well as in my role as a coach, I have answered this question many times: "Am I allowed to say that?" The quick answer is "YES! With some restrictions." If you have looked at the bigger picture, and what you are about to say is in line with the vision, mission, and values, then yes! If you haven't done those things, then step back, take a breath, and think through what you are about to say.

The hard stuff needs to be said, but we don't want to confuse our frustration with a person or a situation with what is right for the business. There will be people on your team who think very differently from you. While it's not your way or your style, it's OK for them to be different, and it could be very helpful for the team to have such different styles. A different style does not necessarily mean "wrong." If their style is different, but it's still pointing people in the direction of the vision and following the mission and values, then it's OK.

When it's not following the vision, mission, and values, that's when we need to have those difficult conversations.

Recently a client was dealing with an employee who had been given everything she'd ever asked for at the company. She was initially in Finance but wanted to move into Production. The company supported her while she returned to school to take the necessary courses to make the move. They then supported her while she tried out the new job but allowed her to keep a part-time role in Finance while she decided if the new role was for her. She then requested to be removed completely from Finance, and again the company supported her choice. After all these moves, for some reason this employee did not feel she had been supported by her managers and would verbalize this to her co-workers on a regular basis. It got so bad that the other employees started making complaints about her. To make matters worse, her immediate supervisor was about to have a surgery that might put him off work for a while.

In my conversation with the manager, we discussed the importance of not leaving the team with this negativity while he was away. We also had concern about the supervisor who would be stepping into the role while he was away. This was not something that she should have to deal with while she was already out of her comfort zone stepping into the leadership role. As uncomfortable as it was, on his last day before heading out for surgery, he had the conversation to explain the expectations while he was away and moving forward. He reminded the employee of all the support she had received, and that the expectation was that if she had an issue with someone on the team, that she takes it up with them directly, not spread rumors in the team.

Unfortunately, this employee still could not see the harm she was doing, nor could she see all the support she had previously received. She chose very shortly after this conversation to leave the company. Had she stayed in her position, the manager would have to have started the discipline process.

Sometimes you will have to ask people to move on from the company or their current role, and sometimes just being clear about expectations, people will move on themselves. Once they know what is expected of them, they will choose to work somewhere where they are a better fit. I have experienced the latter quite often but have also experienced the former. When you come from a place of caring, both for your employees and the company, this process can be made easy.

In my first management role, I worked with an employee who was very close to being terminated. We had followed the disciplinary process right up to the last step. We had attempted to get him help through our Employee Assistance Program, we'd worked with him on how to better manage his time, we'd even bought him a pocket calendar to keep track of his appointments, but it just wasn't working. He was missing appointments with the counselor and continued his "bad behavior" at work.

I was in the middle of working on his termination letter with our lawyer when he came into my office to ask my opinion about something. He had taken two weeks' vacation to try out a new job and was really enjoying the new work. He asked me what he should do. If he chose to leave the company, he would lose all his seniority, vacation time, etc. I told him I couldn't give him advice, but reminded him of how close he was to being terminated and that he would have to be on his best behavior for over a year to ensure he kept all his seniority, etc. During our conversation he came to the decision that he should quit. So together we wrote his resignation letter, and he left the company.

People are shocked when I share this story. Who helps an employee write their resignation letter? Here is the reality of the situation. He was going to be terminated the moment he came back from vacation. I didn't give him advice or tell him he was about to be terminated. I simply reminded him of the reality of his situation with this company. It was all simply facts. With those facts, he made a decision. Since he already had another job lined up, it was better (in my opinion) for him to choose to leave than to be terminated. It never feels good to anyone to be terminated or to do the termination for that matter. Allowing him to choose to leave helped him and the company; it was the "best for project" result.

I have met up with him since this time, and he didn't stay at the new job for long, but he did find something that he really enjoyed shortly afterward and was very happy in his latest role. He didn't fit where we were, and he needed the help to move on. He didn't struggle with any of the things he struggled with at our company in the new role, because he loved what he was doing.

I have also worked with a superior who was new to the company and wasn't meeting the culture. This was at Magna. I had taken six months of training with the company and was very aware of what they did and did not accept from their leaders. I did not report directly to this person, but he would have been considered my superior. He and I regularly argued about what the right decision was on things. Some of these arguments were heated, but never disrespectful. We never called each other names or told each other we were wrong. We stated our case and explained where our choices came from. Many times, the words "That's not the Magna way!" came out of my mouth. Others watching these debates found it uncomfortable, and at times I needed to take a walk to calm down afterward, but we always managed to come to a decision that met the culture and dealt with the situation appropriately. This manager and I had the same personality style. Those heated debates did not bother us; they were productive and respectful. While at times exhausting, we managed to make better decisions because of them.

I shared some of these conversations with a friend who was in the military. He was shocked that I had these conversations with a superior and had not been terminated, or at least disciplined. Again, that was not the Magna way. Magna respects the views of all their employees and expects that if you know something, you speak up.

Yes, you can say that—if it's in line with your vision, mission, and values and you are not reacting to a different style, that while different, is still in line with the company culture. You have also considered what you are going to say. Having a disagreement is always welcome if the disagreement is respectful and productive. The moment it becomes disrespectful and unproductive, it's best to stop and come back when everyone has calmed down.

Chapter 9

Whose Job Is It to Tell Them?

When coaching leaders I often ask, "Did you tell them that was not acceptable behavior?" The answer I hear often is "They should know!" The reality is that people forget, life happens, and emotions get high sometimes, along with a thousand other reasons why people are behaving in a way that doesn't match the culture you are trying to create.

I hear "They should know!" or "They already know!" from both leaders and employees. When I hear it from employees, I remind them that their leader has at times upwards of fifty people reporting to them, and working in a large building, they can't possibly be aware of everything. When I hear it from leaders, I remind them that employees were given several days of training when they first started. They will each remember certain parts better than others, and it's our job to remind them of the expectations.

Some of these situations can become more serious if the conversations aren't had. I once had an employee come to me complaining that her manager had done something sexist. When she relayed the story, it did sound that way, but since I was female, I had experience with this person and had never experienced him being sexist. As a matter of fact, he was generally respectful, sought out, and followed my advice when it was given, which I didn't get from many other managers at this particular job.

The situation was that this woman had recently returned from maternity leave and felt it was time that she have the opportunity to be stepped up into a leadership role and start to practice. The manager told her no because she had just returned from maternity leave. This doesn't seem unreasonable until you compare it to her co-worker, a male, who had just returned from paternity leave and was stepped up very shortly after returning.

The reality was that this woman was not ready to step up into the leadership role, and the manager took what he thought was an easy way out. He used the time away as an excuse not to tell her the full truth.

After discussing the situation and my experience with the supervisor, the employee decided she would confront her manager. She did so very respectfully but did point out to him that his "excuse" was not in line with his own practice, and she stated very plainly that it seemed incredibly sexist. As was expected, he came to me shortly afterward feeling terrible. He relayed the situation, and I shared that she had already discussed it with me. We discussed why he felt she wasn't ready to be stepped up, and then he returned and worked out a plan with the employee so that she knew exactly what was expected of her before she would be considered for a leadership role.

I believe my words, when the manager came into the office to discuss it with me, were "Why weren't you just honest with her in the first place? I almost had to open a human rights investigation against you." His reason was that he didn't want to hurt her feelings. This is another sentence that comes up often. As a leader, you must be honest—respectful but honest in the *behavior* you see and what you expect. In this case, while it was hard for the employee to hear all the reasons that she wasn't ready to be in the leadership role, she could not disagree. She immediately got the support she needed through courses and coaching to be able to step into a leadership role in the future. She was eventually stepped up and started sharing the story of the previous treatment she and other women had received in her field. She had good reason to think that this manager might be sexist; she had been experiencing it since she was in school for her field.

It doesn't always turn out that well. If that manager did not have a good relationship with me, or if I were male, as Human Resources, I would have had to open an investigation. His actions looked sexist considering he was stepping up a male who had also taken paternity leave twice! Why would he only punish the woman for taking time off? Since I was female and he had already established a very respectful relationship with me, I was able to share my experience, and then the employee and I worked together to find a better way to handle the situation. An investigation in this case would have been uncomfortable for both parties. All his reasons for not stepping her up would have been shared with a larger group of people, putting her in an uncomfortable position and he would have been marked in his role by this investigation no matter the outcome.

Sometimes people cannot hear or see anything other than what they initially saw or heard. In the previous chapter, I shared the story about the employee who could not see all the support she'd received from the company, and always felt like she was not being supported in her role. When that happens there is nothing you can do but continue to share how you interpret the situation and ask them to change their behavior. If they cannot, it's up to you as the leader to start the discipline process. At that point they either change their behavior or they will get to the point of termination. The ideal situation is that they change their behavior. If that happens, it's important to let them know that you are seeing the improvements they have made.

The Importance of Being Consistent

I think it's important to take a moment here to discuss consistency. It's important that you are consistent in how you are handling employees' behavior. Consistency does not mean the same. We used the example in the last chapter about two employees being late—one had thirty years' tenure and had never been late, while the other was a recent employee with many lates. While both should be acknowledged, for the former a simple "Is everything OK?" and for the latter more likely a discipline letter at the very least. We have a tendency as leaders to treat those who are most like us more favorably than those who are not. Back to chapter 1 of knowing yourself—you need to be aware of this and make a conscious effort to treat everyone equally.

Consistency also means that no matter what day of the week, inappropriate behavior will be handled the same way. If it's our policy to deal with every latecomer, we deal with all of them. Again, not the same, but they will all be acknowledged and reported to whatever system you use to track these types of events.

This is easier said than done. We have all had those moments in our lives where some minute event that had been happening for months suddenly really makes us angry, like your significant other who leaves their socks on the table. One day you just move them, the next, because of the stress you experienced that day, you find yourself so very frustrated with the socks that you are ready to throw them right at their owner's head! These are the moments we need to realize that we aren't in the right space to deal with the situation and allow ourselves the space to calm down before continuing. Try using a simple sentence like "I'm aware but am choosing to deal with this later today," or "We will discuss this further tomorrow."

Life is going to happen. You need to look at the larger picture and be aware of your own personal energy at the time. You want to remain consistent in how you handle things, but equal doesn't mean the same.

Yes, as a leader it is your responsibility to tell your team whether to start/stop that behavior. Don't assume that they already know or remember all the rules they were given on their first day.

Root Four: Know How to Discuss the Tough Stuff

I hope it has become obvious from the last section that as a leader it's your role to initiate and facilitate the difficult conversations. Some prefer the terms crucial, tough, challenging, painful—feel free to add your own word. These are the conversations that we all stress about, knowing that it's going to be hard to give the message that we must give, and worse, the fear around how the person will react to the message.

In the book *Crucial Conversations*[2], the authors suggest that to be called crucial, the conversation will have three parts:

1. Opposing opinions
2. High stakes
3. Strong emotions

As a leader, this happens regularly. An example is using the disciplinary process or telling an employee that their work wasn't up to par. They may think that they did a good job (opposing opinion), or they may be afraid of losing their job (high stakes), but

---

[2] Joseph Grenny, Kerry Patterson, Ron McMillan, Al Switzler, Emily Gregory, *Crucial Conversations: Tools for Talking When the Stakes Are High, Second Edition* (New York: McGraw Hill, 2012), 1–2.

both of those will create strong emotions for them. For yourself, you feel they need to improve (opposing opinion). Allowing them to continue to do subpar work will bring into question your ability as a leader and cause problems in the team (high stakes), and again both of those will create strong emotions for you.

No matter what you call them or how you feel about them, as a leader you need to get comfortable having these types of conversations. In my experience, the only way to get comfortable is to practice. Unfortunately, with these types of conversations, it's hard to "practice" outside of real-world experience. When I train on this, I have attempted at times to create scenarios and have people role-play through the scenarios. The problem with this is that the emotions aren't there in a made-up scenario. We still do it to have a safe place to practice, but until you are in the real-world conversation, it's hard to know how you will react.

Our emotions are very much present in a difficult conversation. They will be there for us and for the other party. That's expected, and it's OK. In the book *Difficult Conversations*,[3] the authors suggest that attempting to have a difficult conversation without acknowledging the feelings is like going to an opera with no music. The goal is that we become aware of and control our emotions during these conversations, rather than having our emotions control us.

Throughout my career, I've had incredibly difficult and awkward conversations. Here are a few of the topics:

- Staff members' behavior
- Personal hygiene
- Substance abuse

---

[3] Douglas Stone, Bruce Patton, Sheila Heen, *Difficult Conversations: How to Discuss What Matters Most*, Tenth Anniversary Edition (New York: Penguin Group, 2010).

- Employees' health concerns (usually either telling them they weren't ready to work or convincing them it was time to come back to work)
- Working through someone's belief that "management" was out to get them without the understanding that I was management, when they thought I was awesome
- Safety requirements that slowed production, convincing employees their safety was first
- Convincing an employee to put in his resignation when he was about to be terminated
- Terminating someone's employment (this one never feels good, no matter how much you practice)

These are only a few examples. These conversations happened on a regular basis; initially they were not easy for me, but the more I had them, the more comfortable I got with them.

Thankfully, it wasn't me who had to have the discussion about the employee's personal hygiene. One of the supervisors working with me came to my office and informed me that we had an employee who did not smell very nice. We were working in the entertainment business and this employee had lots of interactions with patrons, so this meant a discussion was needed. The supervisor and I discussed the importance of being understanding. Some people just smell more than others. I have friends who never need to wear deodorant because their sweat just does not stink, and I have another friend who would put deodorant on fifteen times a day or more and still smelled like sweat; there was little she could do (though she did eventually get prescription from her doctor that helped). With this information in hand, the supervisor went to have a discussion with the employee. They had a lovely conversation. The hard stuff was said with grace and understanding, and the employee felt safe sharing what was happening in her life. There were some tears because the employee was sharing some pretty tough personal information, but they came up with a plan to help with the situation. The situation was resolved.

Some other important parts to this are that the supervisor did not confront the employee where she might be overheard; she found a quiet space where they would not be disturbed. She also did not share what the employee shared, as far as the personal issues, with anyone else, including me.

In the following chapters we will walk through a framework to prepare yourself, with a mix of the suggestions for how we control ourselves. We will end with some examples and results from these conversations. These types of conversations are never "easy," but you can learn to have them with grace, understanding, and care for both you and the other party.

Chapter 10

How Do I Prepare?

Sometimes a difficult conversation comes to us by surprise, so it's not always possible to prepare. I have two responses when I hear this:

1. You can always ask for space to step back and consider options or take time to understand your own feelings about something.
2. The more you practice, the easier it gets to control your own emotions when the conversation comes by surprise.

Like anything else though, you need to practice first. Where possible, plan the conversation in advance by asking yourself the questions laid out in this chapter. The more you do this, the less often you have to go back to a sheet to figure out the questions you have to ask yourself first.

Before we consider how to prepare for the difficult conversation, it's important to understand a few concepts:

1. Communication model

This is the explanation of how all communication works. There is a sender who encodes a message and a receiver who decodes it. We use the word *medium* to describe how the message is sent because there are so many ways to send a message now: face-to-face, over

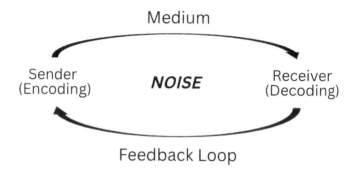

the internet via multiple social media platforms, or email, video calls, etc. Regardless of the medium, there is a feedback loop. Some are better than others. If we are face-to-face, the feedback loop is more immediate, people can see the reactions in our body language and facial features. Things like texting or social media messages have slower feedback or in some cases none at all.

But what we need to focus on in a difficult conversation is the middle part, "NOISE." When I first learned this model, we were talking about actual noise. For example, we are talking and a big truck drives by, it's loud, so we can no longer hear each other. When we are in a difficult conversation, the noise can be that, but it's also so much more. Here are just a few examples:

- Different personalities (discussed earlier in the book)
- Distractions when encoding or decoding (think autocorrect and how many problems that caused)
- Values
- Beliefs
- Culture
- Life experience
- Expectations
- Understanding
- Perception

That's a lot of things that add noise to a conversation or an event. If I have an expectation of how things will go and you have a different expectation, no matter what happens, one or both of us will not be pleased with the outcome unless we have taken the time to discuss our expectations.

Each part of this list can be the beginning of a conflict where we will need to have a difficult or crucial conversation to clarify things.

2. Ladder of Inference

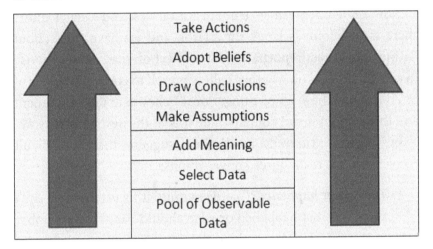

The ladder of inference was created by a man named Chris Argyris, and it explains how humans come to conclusions.

We start at the bottom of the ladder and move up each rung very quickly. Sometimes the whole thing happens as fast as the snap of your fingers. We see only what's in front of us (i.e., "the pool of observable data"). From what we see, we select the data. For example, have you ever bought a new car thinking that you had a fancy color that no one else has, but then all of a sudden you see cars with the same color everywhere? Those cars were there before, you just weren't looking for them, so you didn't see them. Once we have selected the data, we add meaning, make assumptions, draw conclusions, adopt a belief, and take action. (Though hopefully after reading this section, you learn not to act so immediately.)

The best way to explain this is with a story. I used to get my coffee at 10:00 a.m. every day.

At 10:00 a.m. I saw John having coffee with Jane. Initially, I thought nothing of it, but after a few weeks of seeing John and Jane having coffee every day, what might I start to think?

When I do this live, at this point I start getting head nods and smiles. They are thinking like me . . . maybe John and Jane have a deeper relationship or maybe they are even having an affair.

Now remember, I'm in Human Resources, and what I didn't share is that John is Jane's supervisor, and we have rules about dating your direct reports, so I have to act on this. How I choose to act will depend on whether I allow myself to go up the ladder of inference like the snap of a finger or if I choose to take a moment and think about how I could handle this in the best possible way.

In *Difficult Conversations*[4] they suggest that a difficult conversation is really three conversations:

1. **The "what happened?" conversation.** This is where we can't agree on what happened or what should happen. Remember in communication all the different noise, also the ladder of inference. When we see or experience something, we add so many parts of our own existence to the experience that it's not easy to agree on what we saw. This one is also split into three parts:
   a. The truth assumption (we think, *I am right, and you are wrong.*)
   b. The intention invention (we think, *I have good intentions; you do not.*)
   c. Blame frame (we think, *Whose fault is this? Most likely yours.*)

---

[4] Stone, Patton, Heen, *Difficult Conversations*, 7.

2. *The "feelings" conversation.* Hopefully this is more obvious. We have feelings about everything that we see or experience; it's part of our nature. It's also part of our nature to question our feelings—Are they appropriate? Should I acknowledge them? They become part of a difficult conversation whether we mean them to or not.

3. *The "identity" conversation.* This is where we start to look at what this situation says about who we are and what it means for us. We ask ourselves questions about whether we are competent, whether we are behaving as a "good" person, and whether we've made the right decisions. If the answer is "no" to any of these, we won't feel balanced in the conversation; i.e., it will be harder to control our emotions.

Once we are aware of the above, we can start preparing for the conversation by walking through the three conversations[5]:

1. What happened?
   - This is easier said than done. When we tell the story of something that happened to us, we add a lot of layers. Those layers include assumptions, bias, blame, stories about the other person's intentions . . . you add in your own intentions. We are always kinder about our own intentions than we are about other people's intentions. We assume we are good, and they have sinister intentions. So figuring out what happened is not that easy.

Let's use the example I mentioned earlier. What happened with John and Jane? John supervises Jane, and they are having an affair. Um, nope! What happened is that I saw John and Jane having coffee at 10:00 a.m. every day. That's it! The answer to "What happened" tends to be a very short—one to two sentences once we take out everything we've added to it.

---

[5] *Difficult Conversations*, 233.

2. What feelings/emotions is this bringing up for you?

- The simple act of naming your feelings will help to dissipate their strength. When you become aware of what you are feeling, it's easier to control the feeling than allow it to control you.

What was I feeling with John and Jane? Concern and fear. I was worried that they were having an affair and I was going to have to do an investigation, or the worst-case scenario was that John was doing something inappropriate and using his power as a supervisor over Jane. Possibly, I might also feel betrayed if I had a personal relationship with John.

3. What does this situation say about who you are? How will it affect your future?

- Our identity isn't all or nothing; we change all the time. We can consider ourselves compassionate people, but in this particular situation we aren't being very compassionate. We can also be concerned about our future, and what this particular situation will do to our reputation or something tangible like our jobs.

I was feeling like I was failing at my job for not being aware that something like this was happening. Then, because I'd already made the assumptions, when I started walking through the questions, I was feeling like I was judging both John and Jane, when I like to think that I'm not a judgmental person. This brought up feelings of guilt.

I find that questions two and three might create a bit of a circle. When you start thinking about how the situation is affecting your future, you will start to bring up other feelings, and it's important to acknowledge all of them.

Now that I've walked through the questions, I can approach John. Had I not looked at the three conversations, I may have approached John with "What's going on with you and Jane? Are you having an affair with her?"

Now imagine John's reaction, especially if he was a married man who had a strong value for fidelity. He would immediately have his back up and be incredibly insulted that I would think that of him. I'm sure his response would not have been kind, and rightly so.

Once I've gone through the questions, I realize that all I saw was them sitting together every day, so I could choose not to have the conversation, or I might approach John with "Hey, I notice you have coffee with Jane every day—is everything OK?"

Here's the outcome of this story. Yes, John has coffee with Jane every day at 10:00 a.m., but had I changed my time for getting coffee, I'd see that he has coffee with Mike at 10:10 a.m. and Mary at 10:20 a.m. John likes informal meetings with his team and prefers an informal setting like the coffee room so the team isn't intimidated by his office. Remember the "pool of observable data." We only see what we see, and we aren't always there, so we need to be open to accepting other information.

The last thing before we step into a conversation is to decide if having a conversation is the best way to solve the problem. Some things to consider here:

- What do you want for yourself, for the other parties, and for your relationship?
- Will a conversation get you there?
  - o Check your motives for having the conversation.
  - o Is there another way to deal with the issue?
  - o Does the situation even require a conversation?
- If your answers above were true, how would you behave?

When I was first in business, I had rented a room in a city outside of mine. I rented the room for two weeks in a row and had a four-hour presentation to share each day. It was a Saturday, so there was no one else in the building and the door was unlocked and relocked remotely. The only options for the room rental were half-day or full-day. I chose half-day, assuming I could have a few minutes to set up and tear down outside the four hours.

After the first session, one of the participants had some questions. She stayed with me while I cleaned up, and then we chatted for a while. I wasn't concerned because I didn't think I was bothering anyone since the building would be locked remotely, and it wasn't reasonable to step outside in a Northern Ontario winter.

The following week I got a call from the receptionist at the building reminding me that I only had four hours. I was confused because I'd spoken to the owner when I left the week prior. I asked to speak to the owner because the room was not set up when I arrived, so I needed a little time to make sure that I was set up before the clients arrived. Then I would need a little time to tear things down. We went back and forth via text for a while, and I started to get frustrated. Someone suggested that I stop texting and just message the participants letting them know we would start fifteen minutes later than initially suggested. I did that and then shortened the presentation where I could, and we were out in the four hours.

I then went through the three questions:

1. What happened?
   - I rented the room and stayed longer after the first day. (Big change from the explanation I gave at the beginning of this story, right?)

2. What feelings is this bringing up for you?
   - Frustration, because I wanted my presentation to look professional and people watching me set up did not feel professional.
   - Annoyance, because this owner wouldn't work with me to solve the problem. I could have paid for an extra half hour to set up and tear down.

- Confusion, because what did it matter if no one else was in the building?

3. What does this say about our identity?
   - That I'm not a professional businessperson and the clients at the presentation would see that. (This wasn't true; it was just a fear.)
   - This owner thinks I'm taking advantage of her, and she is going to tell people that's the kind of person I am, and they won't want to do business with me. Which brought on a new feeling: fear of losing my business!

Last, but not least: Does this require a conversation? NO! This did not require a conversation. The only reason I would have spoken to her was to protect my identity. I didn't like the space, because it didn't represent my brand, and I had no intention of using it again. I followed her rules the second week and moved on with a new space for further presentations. We didn't need a further relationship, so a conversation was not needed.

Now we know how to prepare ourselves. We have ideally moved away from wanting to be right and simply prove our point to wanting to understand. In the book *Difficult Conversations,* they call this a "learning conversation." If you can make that simple switch in your mind from considering the upcoming conversation a difficult conversation to a learning conversation, it will change the attitude you bring to the table. Now, what do we do during the conversation?

Chapter 11

What Do I Do During the Conversation?

We've worked through our feelings and our concerns about our personal identity, shifting focus from it being a difficult conversation to wanting to learn. Now what?

The authors of *Difficult Conversations* suggest starting from the third story. This is the story that a mediator or other person who doesn't have strong emotions about the situation would see. Then share your purpose or purposes and invite them to join you as a partner.

Let's go back to the example of renting the room, from the previous chapter. Had I decided that I wanted to use the room again, I could have chosen to have a conversation. Imagine the difference between starting the conversation like this:

"You made me uncomfortable when you were insistent on me getting out in four hours for absolutely no reason."

Or

"I want to discuss what happened last weekend. We obviously had different understanding of what the four hours included when I rented the room, and I want to understand your perspective as well as share mine in the hopes of working together again in the future."

The latter would hopefully get a much better response. The former includes blame and accusations. The latter shares that there is a misunderstanding, shares the purpose of the conversation, and invites the other person to join me as a partner.

As a leader, sometimes you are inviting people to a conversation that they have no choice but to be a part of, something like discipline or an investigation. In this case you can give them the option of timing. I would still go through the steps in the previous chapter so that you are in the headspace of learning. However, in the case of discipline you will also need to be clear on the message that you need to give—the specific behavior that isn't acceptable as well as the expected future behavior. When you are dealing with a behavior pattern that isn't acceptable in your organization, remember that it is a behavior that is the problem and NOT the person. The person has other amazing qualities and behaviors, but this specific one they have been displaying needs to be corrected.

Once both parties have decided to be a part of the conversation, we start to explore their story and yours.[6]

- **Listen to understand.** Sometimes we listen to respond. When we are listening to understand, the first thought in our mind is a question, not a counterpoint. Acknowledge the other person's feelings and accusations. Paraphrase to see if you understand what they said. Get curious to figure out how you got to this point.
- **Share your own viewpoint.** During one presentation, I had a manager tell me about an uncomfortable position one of his staff was putting him in. Instead of sharing with her how

---

[6] *Difficult Conversations*, 234.

he felt, he let her continue the behavior. That does not help anything. You need to listen, but you also need to share your viewpoint. This should be easier for you after having done the steps in the previous chapter. You will be able to share more of the facts and separate the feelings and assumptions you have added. That does not mean you don't share the feelings that came up for you, just that you can separate them from the facts.

- *Reframe, reframe, reframe.* In order to stay on track, you may need to reframe some of what is being said. When a perception is being shared, reframe that perception back to the facts, blame to contribution, accusations to feelings, and so on. An example of reframing I often used is when employees would come to me and say negative things about the company "just wanting to make money." I would agree and remind them that we were shareholders so we too wanted the company to make money, plus it was easier for the management team to agree to raises if they had satisfied the shareholders' needs. I also reminded them that the company had a legal requirement to maximize results for the shareholders.

Once we have both shared our stories and taken the time to paraphrase and fully understand each other's viewpoint, we can start to problem solve. To be clear, this does not mean we already have agreement on everything, just that we understand each other's viewpoint. There may be some facts still in dispute that we have to agree to disagree on. That doesn't stop us from moving forward with the problem solving.

When problem solving, I like the idea of spaghetti on the wall. Throw it all on a piece of paper or white board and see what sticks. When I'm mediating a dispute, I even put up the sarcastic answers. Include the ones that start with "Well, if you are going to say that, then we should . . ." More often than I can tell you, these answers, as long as they aren't harmful or mean, make their way into the final decisions.

Once you have exhausted all the options, you can start to cross out the ones that clearly won't work so you are left with all the best options. Sometimes in this process a new idea comes up. That's OK too.

In some cases, you need to find external standards. An easy example is that if something in the dispute has a cost, you can look for similar items. For example, a property. You can look up other similar properties in the area to find a reasonable price. If the dispute is a salary, you can also look up similar salaries to have a standard. These standards need to be agreed on by both parties. If you know in advance, you can ask that the other party have some standards before they enter the discussion, then you bring yours and you find a middle ground.

Once we decide on the final option, it's not done. I always suggest having a time for review. The amount of time will depend on what is being discussed. You need to have a date for review and stick to it. Sometimes in the moment we agree to something, that once we start trying to use it, it does not work in practice. That doesn't mean we give up. We just come back together to talk about what's working and what's not.

This process seems easy, but it requires that we are all honest with ourselves and with the other person. When something doesn't work, we have to be willing to say, "That doesn't work for me" or "I'm uncomfortable with that" or even "That would be outside my values." We also have to be willing to take a break or walk away if we can't control our emotions or if we feel unsafe. Safety does not solely mean physical safety. If the other party becomes abusive in their use of words, then it is acceptable to step away. To be clear, there is a difference between "I don't like when you . . ." or "When you do . . . it goes against our company standards" and calling someone a name, or saying, "It's abusive when you . . ." While the latter is not exactly calling someone a name, it's naming the behavior in a very negative light.

Sometimes It Isn't Pretty

I had an employee whose role was Publicity, but he reported to me in Human Resources. I didn't know his job; my experience was all in Human Resources. I was also around half his age, but that wasn't the issue. You see, he could retire at any moment. I kept asking him his plans, and he thought it was funny not to tell me his plans. He ignored the question or made some joke about it. I started learning everything I could about his job. This looked like me asking him where he was going and why. Eventually he took this to mean I didn't think he knew how to do his job.

One day he came in my office very upset and almost yelling at me. "Lisa, I have never been treated this way in the thirty years I have been doing this job. You're constantly questioning me and my ability to do this job."

Maybe not my best moment but my reply was "Bullshit! I have been asking you since I got here what your plan is for retirement. You think it's funny not to tell me. I have never done publicity and since you won't tell me, I decided I have six months to learn your job to be prepared to replace you properly!"

That stopped him. He looked stunned, but immediately calmed down. I don't remember the rest of the conversation verbatim, but I know it was a much calmer one. He understood finally why I was asking so many questions, and I understood why he could not tell me when he would retire (he didn't know). We came up with the plan that he would come and see me every Friday and explain what he had done that week and why it was important.

This wasn't an easy conversation for either of us. We both had to be vulnerable and share our truths. If we hadn't, I imagine it would have been a very uncomfortable relationship. I imagine he might have retired sooner just to get away from me! We both shared, we both listened, and I know that I had to reframe his belief that I was "questioning" him so that he understood I was simply trying to understand.

Sometimes the conversation doesn't look pretty. The example above started with a man yelling and I could see tears in his eyes, and me swearing at the beginning of my sentence, but that's not what matters. We were not disrespectful; we did not call each other names or accuse the other of being a bad person in some way. We stuck to the behavior we were seeing from each other and moved forward.

I've also had examples from people taking the "Leading with Ease" course where I ask how the conversation went. They say, "Terrible." When I ask for the explanation, the reality is it was not terrible—they actually resolved the issue. It felt "terrible" because the other person started to cry. There is nothing wrong with someone crying. Crying is simply a stress release. If they can continue the conversation with understanding, just move forward, though always offer a tissue and to take a break if they need it. This doesn't mean break for a day; this means a few minutes to collect themselves.

This is all easier said than done. Why is it so important to do this? We examine this in the next chapter.

Chapter 12

What Good Can Come of This?

There is a reason the difficult/crucial or learning conversations come as the last root. We talked about knowing what you want in the preparation of the conversation. We also talked about taking time to work through your own feelings and the importance of controlling your feelings during the conversation rather than allowing them to control you. Some of these pieces are discussed in the previous roots.

What we want is in our mission, vision, and values. How to conduct ourselves and control our emotions come from the first root, "Knowing ourselves." What needs to be discussed comes from Root Three, Know Your Role. If you are aware of all the previous roots, Root Four becomes much easier. What you want is clear, your knowledge of your own strengths and weaknesses is clear, and the expectations of your team are already set out.

How does this help us? The better we get at having difficult conversations, the better information we will have when it's time to make a decision or choose a path. The better the team gets at these conversations, the more comfortable they will feel with providing a dissenting opinion. When you and the team are making a decision, you always want a dissenting opinion. This makes sure that someone is seeing things in a different light and allows you to see all sides of a situation.

There is a famous story about John F. Kennedy after making a very poor decision known as "The Bay of Pigs Fiasco." Kennedy changed the way his team made decisions. *Harvard Business Review* sets out four steps that Kennedy put in place,[7] however it doesn't have to be as complicated as that. When it was taught to me, they said that Kennedy assigned a "devil's advocate," someone at the meeting whose job it was to provide a dissenting opinion to any ideas that had been put forward. This ensured that the team avoided what we call "groupthink." Groupthink happens when a team is focused on consensus at all costs and avoids dissenting thoughts and an actual review of alternative ideas. If we are going to avoid groupthink, we need our teams to be comfortable with difficult conversations.

In my first full-time role, I had been brought in after spending six months training at head office. This made my co-workers believe that I was "help" from head office, and it was not looked at kindly. To make matters worse, my boss had been assigned as "help" from head office, so trying to convince others that I was not in the same position was not easy. There was a human resources manager and two generalists. I was one of the generalists, but the other generalist did not trust me. It took months, but finally we were assigned a project together, and because we worked at different buildings, we decided that we would meet at a restaurant to work on the project. This made all the difference, because it was an informal setting where it felt more comfortable to be honest. During our lunch, she realized that I thought the same way she did, and we had a lot of the same concerns about what was happening at our workplace. We also had the same concerns about some of the leaders, but we had very different approaches. This led to more

---

[7] https://hbr.org/2013/11/how-john-f-kennedy-changed-decision-making.

conversations, and it allowed me to bring some of the concerns from the rest of the team to my boss. They weren't exactly open with her. From that my boss changed the way we handled things. While she and I did not need a spreadsheet with all the upcoming projects, the rest of the team felt better with one, so we assigned one of the admins to create one. Something so simple changed the way the team thought of my boss, and suddenly the team started to open up about their concerns. Now we were able to talk about our thoughts on decisions that were being made and our choices got much better. When everyone is comfortable sharing their views, the decision making improves immensely. That generalist and I have stayed friends. It's been seventeen years since I left that role. It's amazing the difference one lunch can make.

At that same company we got a new assistant general manager. It was a role that hadn't existed at this company prior, and the general manager didn't feel there was anyone ready at the company that could take the role. While this person was great at organizing and helping the team see the bigger picture, he was not the strongest at the difficult conversations mostly because he wasn't the best at listening. He also wasn't the best at following the culture that this company had worked so hard to create.

This created many issues and somehow, even though I was a generalist and technically he would have been a superior, I ended up being the person who could speak to him so that he understood. Consequently, my boss and some of his direct reports would invite me into meetings when they needed him to understand something. He and I had the same personality, so we could match each other's energy. Sometimes these conversations didn't look pretty, and others might get uncomfortable with the level of enthusiasm we both brought, but they worked. With this assistant general manager, you needed to be clear and repeat yourself several times. For me that sometimes meant sharing my opinion forcefully, partially because I was annoyed that I was saying the same thing for the fourth time in a conversation and he still hadn't gotten it. I want to be clear, while I was frustrated with this person, he wasn't a bad person. He wanted what was best for the company, but he was doing it with the knowledge he had gained working in a different culture. We needed the time to have him understand our culture. It wasn't easy but we got there. The sentence I remember repeating to him the most was "We don't do that here; our values state . . ." Staying consistent in the values is what allowed us to help this man get to where he needed to be. The general manager, the rest of the managers, and myself all gave him the same messages repeatedly. Once he got it, the decision making was much better in line with the company values.

It doesn't always work out perfectly. I was also on a negotiations team where we were preparing a final offer. Something the union asked for would not be a big deal if we managed to get the rest of the contract dealt with, but it would be a bigger deal if the company ever sold this portion of the company or if they ever had to shut down. The team was exhausted, and we just wanted to be done. One of our team members pointed out the dangers of allowing the language into the contract, but in our exhaustion we didn't take him seriously. It came back to bite the company when a few years later they had to close the doors. They had to close them sooner because we had allowed this clause, and they needed the money to be able to pay what the clause stated. Had we listened more carefully to my colleague's concerns, everyone would have worked longer, and they would have had more time to possibly find a buyer or some other solution to keep this plant running.

As a leader it's important not to shy away from difficult conversations. It's so important to allow your team to share their opinions even if they are contrary to yours. It not only helps you make better decisions, but it allows the team to feel as though their thoughts and opinions matter. This will increase motivation and decrease turnover. Many studies have been done through the years about what makes an employee stay with an organization. Most people are surprised to hear that money rarely makes the top of the list. It's in there, but it's way down the list. At the top of the list are things that deal with job satisfaction and company culture. There have been so many studies that it's hard to say exactly what is at the top, but usually some version of feeling valued, recognized, and respected are in the top two. If they don't feel like anyone is listening when they speak, then those things will not be present.

Knowing ourselves, where we are going, what our role is, and how to have those tough conversations puts us in a really great position as a leader. Having those as roots allow us and our teams the opportunity to stay rooted but bend and shift when the world changes. We all know how quickly the world changes now. As leaders, it's important that our teams feel grounded but are able to be flexible to deal with whatever the world throws at us.

Putting It All Together

We have the four roots: Know Yourself, Know the Destination, Know Your Role, Know How to Discuss the Tough Stuff. Hopefully now you are better rooted in your leadership role. This will allow you to have a solid foundation but still bend and shift with changing technologies and world views. What does that even look like?

In this last section, I share some stories that help to put it all together. They are stories from previous attendees of "Leading with Ease," a few more from my previous career, and a more in-depth of what Cementation went through to create their culture. The first section shares the story from a company I worked at that went through the pain of trying to change a very ingrained culture. It's a lot easier said than done and why I feel it is so important that when starting your business, you are clear on your vision, mission, and values. Creating a culture is a lot easier than changing one.

No matter how prepared you are or how solid your foundation, when you are in a leadership role, you will have some difficult situations to handle. As the leader you cannot hide from them. Instead get back to your roots and find creative solutions to whatever situation you find yourself in. If you can only come up with one solution, you are likely in a stressed state. Do something to get yourself out of it so that you can come up with at least two solutions before deciding how to handle it. Talk to your team; just because you are the leader does not mean you are alone. It can feel lonely at times being the person with the last say, but if you are listening to your team, you will find those decisions easier to make.

Chapter 13

Culture Change

In my first management role, I worked for an international company based in Canada. Their facilities were in small towns across the globe. The management of the company were wonderful people to work with. They were so personable. You never felt like you had to mind your Ps and Qs when the CEO showed up. He was always genuinely interested in you as a person and listened carefully to what you had to say no matter your position in the organization. The rest of his team followed suit.

They weren't as clear on their vision and mission as Magna or Cementation. They had their vision, mission, and values, but they were not as good at marketing it to their employees. It became more of the "words on a wall" than a living and breathing document. They had safety policies, and they worked very hard to make sure that their employees were working safely. Policies, procedures, celebrations for no lost time milestones. Regular sharing of incidents between countries and plants. Regular auditing of the safety programs.

Not long after I arrived, there was a series of accidents that showed that all the work that had been put in on safety policies and rewards were not working. There had been a death in one plant group. We shared the results of the investigation immediately so that no other plant group could have this problem. Within months (i.e., less than three months later), there was another death at another plant group. The two died in the exact same way.

This was followed shortly afterward by one of the company experts being crushed in a machine that he was the expert on. He was crushed after sending a less-senior staff member to get the proper safety equipment. They had no explanation for this one. He knew what he was doing and was aware of how to keep the other employee safe that day. It seemed he forgot to tie something off.

At this point the company knew that they had to give breath to those safety documents. This was NOT acceptable to anyone. They needed a culture change. The culture prior to this effort was one they called "cowboy." Everyone just got the job done. They were focused on production and made sure that they got the most product out every day. That was doing a "good" job. Keep the production going and do what you must to make sure that happens. This resulted in people taking unnecessary risks with safety.

I was invited to a meeting held in the United States. I was brought in with other employees from all levels of the organization and every country we worked in. There was a member of the C-suite there, but he mostly listened to what those of us at the plant level had to say. It was clear that some countries took the safety more seriously, but that the whole company needed to be involved in the change.

This group had an amazing time together. Throughout the day we worked hard discussing the topic at hand, but then came together in the evenings to enjoy our time together. We had a few drinks and sang karaoke and took the time to "gel" as a team.

I was shocked at some of what was said during these meetings— things like supervisors knowing how long it takes to safely lock our equipment when there is a jam, then saying nothing when the jam was cleared in less time than it takes to lock the machine out safely. This meant people were entering live equipment, something that we all knew was a recipe for disaster. Regional managers going behind guards on their visits to site. On top of putting themselves in danger they were showing the employees that safety was not important.

Having just left a company where safety was the norm, I was shocked to hear these things and I asked, "Why are these people still working here?" People were then shocked by my statement and there was some debate to which I responded, "Since when is it not OK to say, 'If you don't work safely, you don't work here'?" I later heard the CEO use a statement like this during the roll out. He was making it clear that we were moving forward with this, and it was no longer acceptable to work unsafely or show disregard to the policies, no matter your level in the organization.

It was decided that if anything was going to change, the supervisors needed to be the ones leading the change. A supervisor is the face of the company and if they aren't onboard with safety, no one will be. This is where my definition of leadership came from.

The US session was run by a consultant who was then charged with the task of creating a supervisor training program to help change the culture. Part of the training was going to be to create the same "gelling" that we had at the initial sessions. Supervisors from all over the company were flown to our head office in Toronto. They had a meal together and evening festivities to "gel," and then spent the next few days learning about the changes that we wanted to see in the company.

The change did not happen overnight, and like any other change, some people didn't stay. As always, some chose to leave and others were asked, but the numbers of people dying on our watch was decreased substantially. I left that company two years after this training, and there were no further deaths in that time. My understanding is that they did not have any more after I left either. There were still accidents, but the severity also dropped, and the reporting increased. Which was exactly what they were looking for.

There was a lot of company expense put into this. Hundreds of supervisors were flown in from all over the world to receive this training. It was decided it needed to be done this way to show the importance, and to let the supervisors from different countries have an opportunity to learn from one another and form a bond across the company.

This story has so many great lessons in leadership:

- The C-suite leaders paid attention to their safety stats. They did not try to hide them or push them aside. They recognized their failing and knew they had to do something.

- Those same leaders recognized that they were not the experts. They went to their staff to get a better understanding of what was going on and how they felt it should be fixed.

- They listened! Some of what was said in those meetings was hard to hear. There were pointed remarks at the leaders and where they had failed. Hearing that, leaders at every level of the organization put their egos aside and decided to do better.

- They got the help they needed to make the change, and they put their money where their mouth was. It was not cheap flying every supervisor across countries and oceans, but they knew that safety needed to be a priority. I can assure you those were not easy conversations when the shareholders asked about the expenses.

Changing a culture takes way more effort than starting with a well-thought-out vision, mission, and values. When you pay attention to your culture from the beginning and stay aware of what is and is not working, you are less likely to run into the big problems that this company found themselves in.

Chapter 14

Stories to Bring It All Together

Now that we have all the roots, I wanted to share some stories that pull the roots all together. Some are from experiences I've had, and others are from clients who have come back after taking the course for further coaching and just needed some extra advice.

How Do We Decide?

I had a client take the "Leading with Ease" program. She and her business partner took it together. They wanted to have a good foundation for their business as they started hiring people. They were both very pleased with what they had learned. They actually took the time to create a vision, mission, and values in that section of the course and were doing what they could to work toward it. One day, I got a call from one of the partners. They couldn't agree on something. She went on to share her thoughts on the situation, then shared her business partner's thoughts in as much detail as her own. They just couldn't get to a decision. They had decided to review their notes prior to calling. They reviewed the "difficult conversations" section and couldn't figure out what they were missing.

They weren't missing anything. They had simply reviewed the wrong section. They were already doing very well with all they had learned in the difficult conversation section. They had both shared their concerns and thoughts, the issue was deciding what path to take. For that they needed to go back to their mission, vision, and values and decide which path took them closer to it. Once they did that, the way became clear. My understanding is that the final decision had parts of each of their suggestions.

In this case, the partners were already very much in line with each other on most of what they were doing, all they needed was a reminder of that scene at the end of the road to decide what was best for them.

Top of Mind

Another client who also attended "Leading with Ease" decided to run the course with her entire staff of supervisors a couple of years later. When I do the session with teams, we do a shortened version of the vision, mission, and values section, because there is no need to create them; the company has them in existence. The lesson is more about what it means for each of the leaders at the session. In this case, I started to read the vision and the whole group recited it with me. Then they finished with a second part that I was not aware of. I was shocked, but happy to hear this. I laughed and asked, "What just happened?" Since the manager had already taken the course when we had discussed the importance of regularly reviewing the vision, she had started reciting the vision statement at their weekly meetings. This was something I had shared that was done at Toastmasters meetings. They read the mission at the beginning of the session so that it is in everyone's mind for the meeting. This group had gotten used to reciting it together. They did complain, though, that just reciting it was starting to take away the meaning. So I suggested that they have one person read it each meeting and then have them talk about how the vision or mission would affect their behavior that week or a story of theirs of the vision/mission in action from the week prior. This allowed the vision and mission to stay top of mind, but also added some context to it and added the opportunity for storytelling.

When we start a new plan, we have to take time later to review it. While the suggestion from Toastmasters was helpful at the beginning, after a while it was not working for this team anymore. When that happens, it is important that everyone be able to share their thoughts on what they are doing. This is harder than it sounds. I assume that the fact they shared it had less meaning, because the opportunity arrived when they took a half day for training and I asked the question. My suggestion is to then take time with your team to review what has become your normal and if it is or is not working.

Take Time to Review and Regroup

This is a good suggestion for your own life as well. Sometimes we start something. And it is useful for a time but after a while needs to be reviewed. A good example of this came for me when my stepchildren moved in. I changed my morning routine. I would get up at 6:00 a.m. and come straight to my home office. Then I would be in the kitchen with them as they got ready for school. Once they left, I would do my self-care routine which included meditating, a walk, a small workout, and showering, etc. After a while this did not work anymore. The problem started when clients wanted to meet at 9:00 a.m. This did not give me any time for my self-care routine, and I never ended up picking it up later in the day. A self-care routine is important when you are running a business and suddenly the main parent to two preteens. I realized this was not working because my behavior was not what I wanted it to be and went back to starting the day with my personal routine. I was still around for the kids but was also taking care of myself.

The same happened through COVID-19 lockdowns. While I had been working from home for years already, the addition of both kids being at home became difficult, and I had to review my routines. They were teens, so it was not as difficult as some of my friends who had young kids. They took care of themselves, but when I would take a break for a snack or lunch, suddenly I was free game, and they all needed something. It took a while to notice, but I realized that I never had any downtime. Where my lunches used to be a quiet time for myself to read or watch a funny show, suddenly lunchtime was supporting someone in either their school journey or just dealing with life in general. I needed to reconsider my routines so there was some time that was just for me in the middle of the day. I started to take my lunch with a book outside on a swing. It was perfect. The kids left me alone because my face was in the book. I was still available while I was preparing my lunch, but part of that time was just for me, and I was able to return to work after lunch in a much more focused way.

It is important to regularly review your habits as well as the team habits, but sometimes we have a review because something happens that surprises us, and we need to take the time to really review our values before we make a final decision. This happened at Magna, and it is a story that was shared with me on several occasions.

The Worm Farmer

Magna had a belief in the entrepreneurial spirit. They felt that people with that spirit had more drive to do better with the company. They set up their plant groups in that way. While the plants were under Magna's heading and had to follow the culture, they were otherwise on their own to produce their own innovations. There was sharing of best practices, etc., but each general manager was expected to run the organization like it was his/her own business. At one of the plants an employee was caught with a watering hose out the back door of the plant. He was watering a section of dirt behind the factory. When he was questioned, they found out that this had been going on for some time. This man had a worm farm out back and was making sure that the worms had a good moist area to grow and multiply. He would then go out, pick the worms, and sell them on the weekends or after his shifts.

Now, for many companies this would be immediate dismissal. This man was using company property and water on top of stealing time from his work to water the worms instead of getting his job done.

Magna in their wisdom remembered that they believe in the entrepreneurial spirit and that is exactly what this man was. He was an entrepreneur. He saw a way to make money, and he worked to make it happen. While they could not continue to let him use his work time or use the land and water for free, they made a deal that allowed him to continue his business but also ensured that he was paying his way. They charged him a rental for the use of the land and water but made sure he promised not to use his work time to deal with the worms. He could stay at work late or arrive early as long as someone was aware that he was there so there were no safety concerns.

I love this story. It is such a great example of a company staying true to who they are. Magna believed in the entrepreneur, so terminating someone who was exactly that would not have fit their values very well. Instead, they went with a very surprising option and allowed him to keep his job and his side business.

Joe the Supervisor

Magna was amazing at sharing the stories that mattered. They had another story about "Joe the Supervisor" that I share often, and many people have let me know how much this story affected them. Now, I cannot change the name when I do it because so many people have come to me to talk about "Joe the Supervisor."

In case it's not obvious, Joe was a supervisor at Magna. Joe was loved by his team, and they always did great work for him. Like any great supervisor, Joe was promoted, and the team got a new supervisor. Magna did employee opinion surveys every year. The new supervisor, while well liked, never got the scores on the survey that Joe did. Since Magna is a learning organization, they wanted to know what this meant. They went to the staff and asked them. All they would get was "The new guy is nice, but he is no Joe." This came from more than one person, and the same line was repeated: "He is no Joe." Magna kept trying to figure it out. They even went to Joe and asked what he had done, wondering if maybe he brought in gifts, gave them extra breaks, or maybe extra time off—anything that would make them like him so much more. Joe could not answer either. This went on for a while, and they kept going back to ask Joe if he had come up with anything. One day Joe finally offered the following:

> The only thing I can think of is that when I handed out the pay stubs, I took a moment to thank a couple of people each week for something they had done that week. For example, someone who cleaned up a particularly tough mess I would say, "Thanks for taking care of that," but I only did it for a couple of people each week. I had over fifty reporting to me.

That was all that it took. Do the math on that. If he only acknowledged two out of fifty people in a week, it might take all year before you were acknowledged again, but that was enough. The simple act of acknowledging a job well done was all it took for his staff to give him such great marks on the survey and work that much harder for him.

Sometimes we get too busy trying to figure out the best strategy to motivate people, and all it takes is a simple acknowledgment when a job is well done.

Being a leader means being able to step back and review where you are. As leaders we need to remind ourselves to "get on the balcony." By this I mean, finding a way to step back and take a view of the whole picture. Sometimes it means making a surprising decision because while the situation might seem wrong, it actually meets your values well. Sometimes it means taking a look at our current habits and noticing that they aren't working, and we need to make a change.

Chapter 15

Cementation: A Case Study

Cementation's vision was created on day one of the company's existence because of the need for a business plan. The vision came from President Roy Slack's experience at another consulting firm. The firm was working on a major project that was over budget and behind schedule but was profitable for them. The client proposed a different approach in which the firm would increase their responsibility and their accountability. Roy felt this would be a great partnership model that would create a long-term relationship with the client, but the firm's executive did not want to change the current highly profitable contract, which was at the expense of the client, of course. When Roy formed Cementation, he wanted to make sure there was a clear vision and mission to focus on doing the right thing for the project and fostering mutually beneficial long-term relationships as opposed to short-term gains.

About six years in, it became clear to Roy that while some of the vision, mission, and values were clear to people, other parts were not as clear as they could be, including the concepts of "bias for action" and "best for project" in the mission and values. Realizing that the vision and mission would never be fulfilled if they were not felt "at the face," Roy created a manifesto entitled "The Cementation Way." It was a thirty-eight-page document that he wrote and was published professionally with the help of a marketing firm. The manifesto included a longer explanation and examples of what the vision, mission, and values all meant.

This document was shared with all employees, but the focus was on the supervisors and project managers. It was translated into three different languages to support the provinces and countries where Cementation was working. It was even used in project bids. This is not uncommon. Where Cementation took it a little further is that it was discussed at the annual strategy sessions, discussed at project meetings as well as used when reviewing Cementation's extensive safety programs.

Like Magna, Cementation also did an extensive annual employee survey to address the values, and they too understood that while it was important to do the survey, it was just as important to action the information that came out of the surveys. They watched for trends or big changes in scoring.

Roy also took every opportunity to share ideas and stories about the "best for project" philosophy and the vision to change the industry, especially regarding safety. He looked for aspects of the vision and mission that aligned and resonated with staff and clients and took every opportunity to share how that was being actioned in the organization. In his words, "Every meeting is an opportunity to ingrain your values, but you need to have some creativity to keep it fresh."

One of the stories he shared with me was about a project in Mexico where there was a problem with the mine shaft. There were two ways to fix it: One was more costly to Cementation but made the most sense for the project in the long term. They went with that one. They could have chosen the less-costly option and the client likely would have been pleased at the time, but in the long run the client may have had to redo the work at some point. He also shared a YouTube video where they parodied a Molson commercial (I am Canadian) about being Canadian but made it about Cementation (We Are Cementation).

I met Roy through Toastmasters, a nonprofit international organization that operates clubs worldwide for the purpose of promoting communication, public speaking, and leadership. Cementation has a "corporate club," which basically meant that in order to be a member of this club, you had to work at Cementation. They met every other week, and anyone at the organization was able to join. I was able to visit their meetings because part of my role as our area and division director was to support the club's growth. Roy used his speeches at Toastmasters as an opportunity to instill the company's vision, mission, and values. They also added something different from other Toastmasters clubs. At the Cementation Toastmasters club, there was a safety moment when one of the meeting participants got up to share something about the importance of safety in the workplace or at home. While this wasn't part of Toastmasters, it was another way that Cementation promoted its values.

In our discussion I pressed Roy on how they ensured the manifesto was helping to make changes. He shared that the business development team, the group that were writing proposals, needed to really understand, buy in, and eventually sell the concepts outside the organization. This team became important advocates of the manifesto. Different departments focused on different elements of the manifesto and shared stories about where the manifesto affected them the most. For example, in operations (the people planning and executing the work), they focused on the idea of a "best for project" philosophy. They shared a story where a team developed and proposed a "best for project" design with a client who was initially reluctant, but finally managed to convince them even though it took over a year to do so! They describe it as an example of how patience and perseverance pay off when you believe in a "best for project" approach.

You can see from all the above that sharing the culture isn't a one-and-done event. As a leader it's something that you need to focus on as often as you can.

Not all new ideas work, though. Roy also shared a story of a best practice they heard about at an Employer of Choice conference. A presenter at the conference shared that they had whiteboards in the bathroom for employees to brainstorm and write comments. Their teams would use it when they had an idea, and it would stay there for others to comment on or continue the idea. Cementation tried this concept as well. It did not work out as planned. Instead of new ideas, employees were writing inappropriate things. Instead of sticking with it and trying to force it, the whiteboards were removed immediately. Sometimes you must let go of a plan that isn't working.

Roy created this vision himself. While the world suggests that everything should happen by committee, Roy believes that the vision should come from the leader, otherwise the vision loses the passion behind it. When a leader has a true vision for change, that passion can be felt when it's shared. When a committee is involved, the focus is more about creating by consensus, and it loses its passion. The committee is best used for policy and procedure creation, but the vision needs to have the passion of the person who created it.

Roy also shared a book he put together called *Observations in Leadership, Horrible Bosses, Go Fever, and Other Leadership Stories and Observations.* On page 64 of the second edition, Roy shares the following about competition:

> We model ourselves after our vision and mission and values. We must always respect our competition, but also recognize that their goals are most likely different than ours. That being the case, modeling our services, bidding strategy, and other aspects of our operations based on what our competition is doing probably won't align us with our own goals. Your strategy needs to be aligned with the "Why," with what you believe in.

I immediately earmarked this page, because I believe that this is an important statement for the company as a whole, but also for each leader. I cannot lead as Roy does because I'm not Roy. Roy cannot lead as I do because he is not me. We each need to take the best parts of ourselves and bring them forward. It's OK if it doesn't look like what the manager next to you is doing. If you are modeling, teaching, creating, and developing that commitment to personal responsibility, you are doing your job.

CPSIA information can be obtained
at www.ICGtesting.com
Printed in the USA
BVHW052015301222
655315BV00014B/1715